INDIGENOUS KNOWLEDGE TRADITIONS

INDIGENOUS KNOWLEDGE TRADITIONS

Perspective from North East India

Edited by

Sarthak Sengupta

GYAN

Indigenous Knowledge Traditions :
Perspective from North East India

ISBN : 978-81-212-1156-7

Published in 2012 in India by
Gyan Publishing House
23, Main Ansari Road, Daryaganj,
New Delhi - 110002
Phones : 23282060, 23261060
Fax : (011) 23285914
E-mail: books@gyanbooks.com
website: gyanbooks.com

Laser Type Setting : Rajender Vashist, Delhi
Printed at : Chawla Offset Printers, Delhi

Dedicated to
the memory of
Late Professor Asok K. Ghosh

Contents

List of Tables

List of Tables

Preface

The seven sister states of North East India are home to rich cultures, nature-friendly traditional technologies and enduring social institutions. It is said that more than 275 indigenous ethnic groups inhabit the region. The region has been traditional habitat of highest diversity of ethno-cultural groups mostly having Mongoloid ethnic strains. Living close to the nature, the people of the region are familiar with the natural resources. They represent a vast assortment of sound ecological and biological knowledge, an invaluable library, that is gradually faded away or being destroyed every year. Many of this indigenous knowledge is unknown by the world outside.

The inhabitant of the region mostly practise *jhuming*, hunting, trapping or collect plants and animals for medicines, ornaments, decoration and supplementing food. These practices are associated with their agriculture, festivals, mythology, rites and many other activities. There are certain cultural totems, and taboos and ethos, which restrict the hunting or killing certain animals and cutting certain plants. By empirical reasoning and trial and error, they have screened and developed a highly complex and very specific knowledge of local resources and its sustainable utilisation. These traditional methods play an important role in conservation and management of natural resources for sustenance.

Indigenous knowledge may be defined as the participant's knowledge of their temporal and social space. It is local but need not always be traditional. It is practical and related to operational local thinking in such fields as technology, agriculture, health, etc. Indigenous knowledge is widely known by the people, the community, or the region and may effectively be used for the uplift of the community. It encompasses non-technical insights, wisdom, ideas, perceptions and innovative capabilities. The ethnic groups of North East India as elsewhere retain a great deal of indigenous knowledge, expertise, institutions and technology that they evolved in order to cope with the ecological imperatives. The people of this region still make ample use of indigenous knowledge in their day-to-day activities, in the domain of agriculture, health, animal and plant-lore etc. Recently, we noticed the awakening of the concept namely, that traditional knowledge of primitive people reveals wisdom that we should better not ignore.

Study reveals that historically operational knowledge has long preceded scientific knowledge. The arrowheads used by the tribes, for instance, are indeed technological marvels. The designs as we see today did include aerodynamic considerations. Perhaps over a period, through hit and miss methods they learnt that the shape and trajectory of arrows are interrelated.

Several ethnic groups of North East India are biochemists of no mean order. The knowledge of preparing a poison tipped arrow, use of alkaloids for fishing are some of the examples. Some of this poison is cardiac stimulant too. As a result, when the arrow strikes the prey, the heart works fast and the poison circulated quickly. Interestingly, at the time of hunting, there is a sense of these people of being part of the nature, part of the same fabric that intertwines men, plants and animals. There is no cruel pleasure, no over kill. Their culture considers oneself as a part of nature. Many ethnic groups even request the God to pardon their clan member for having forced to kill animals or cut down certain trees.

In the field of agriculture, many tribes used compost as manure and had surprisingly accurate knowledge of plant ash as a supplementary fertiliser. The traditional practices like crop rotation, habitat manipulation, windbreak, snail as well as pest control, etc. were far more effective than today's modern methods in this regard. System of land management is also democratic and effective in land control. Construction of indigenous irrigation canals and earthwork embankments for diverting water from riverbed to rice field is also traditional practice of many Bodo speaking tribes of Lower Assam. Many tribes of Arunachal Pradesh have traditional flour mills operated by water power for grinding wheat, barley, millet, etc. into a fine flour which is cooked in water and eaten as a kind of paste. These mills are self-operated by waterpower and require minimum watch, a function that is mostly carried out even by an old man. The vast array of rice strains developed in North East India, more than 5000 varieties alone from Assam are kept in International Rice Research Institute. Selective breeding over centuries created special varieties. Some of the varieties are resistant from pests, diseases and adverse weather conditions. Instant rice – *Komal Chaul* in Assam is a unique variety, which serves a quick meal. The ethnic groups of the region have a very rich knowledge on edible plants also. In North East India, about 300 plant species are consumed as food plants. Indigenous knowledge of the Mizo tribe that the exponential rise in rodent population with the onset of bamboo flowering has a close association with the severe famine *Moutam* which usually occurs after every 50 years or so.

In North East India, a form of forest management did exist even before the British as policy makers formulated a national forest policy. Sacred groove are a significant feature in most of the tribal villages of North East India even today. These grooves are natural treasure houses of plants and animals preserved through ages and are excellent manifestations of traditional wisdom. The forests of North East India are believed to be storehouses of medicinal plants and all the ethnic groups of the region recognise the value of such plants, mixed their ideas with myth and beliefs in gods and demons. Time has come to validate this wisdom scientifically.

In recent years, there is slow but gradual erosion of this indigenous knowledge due to factor and forces of exogenous change. There is an urgent need therefore for documentation of this knowledge to inventories the skills and techno-economic capacities of communities that can be utilised in developing the indigenous economy and environmental security of habitat in a sustainable way. Many of this crude knowledge can be utilised in developing new technology. Indigenous knowledge system needs to be viewed as complimentary to scientific base system. A synthesis of traditional knowledge and modern scientific outlook is necessary to evolve a method for improvement of indigenous knowledge. It should not be undermined as local knowledge.

Although the subject Indigenous Knowledge Traditions has assumed great scientific and practical importance, there has been no general, up-to-date account on indigenous knowledge tradition, particularly on the people of North East India available for some years. The present edited volume endeavours to supply this deficiency. The impressive collection of eighteen research articles accommodated in this small treatise offer discrete descriptions on the indigenous knowledge traditions found among the ethnic groups of North East India. The articles included in this volume are the results of serious research and study by social scientists. Obviously, the present treatise does not claim to cover the entire perspectives within its limited space. It touches upon only some important segments of the vast and varied area of the canvass. I would consider my humble effort as a success if the present volume provokes even a single researcher to venture the exploration of the hitherto almost unexplored area of indigenous knowledge traditions in North East India. This area provides immense possibilities for serious research.

The book is dedicated with deep respect to the memory of Dr Asok K. Ghosh, former Professor of Department of Anthropology, University of Calcutta, Kolkata who always inspired and encouraged me during his lifetime. It is impossible to relieve myself of his debt in my professional career.

May 2012 **Sarthak Sengupta**

Acknowledgements

The articles included in this volume were presented at a National Seminar on the *Indigenous Knowledge Traditions* organised by the Department of Anthropology, Dibrugargh University in 2004. I personally owe a debt of profound gratitude to all those scholarly contributors for kindly responding to our request and readily contributing to this volume through their articles.

It has been possible for me to continue my academic pursuit because of the infrastructural facilities provided by the authorities of Dibrugarh University. I avail of this opportunity to express my thanks. I am equally thankful to my colleague Dr M. N. Dutta, Department of Anthropology, Dibrugarh University who helped me in more than one way towards the preparation of this volume. I am particularly fortunate in having the direct assistance from Mrs. Nilanjana Barua in the preparation of the typescript and in seeing it through the press.

I am deeply grateful to my wife, Kaveeta, and to my children, Sushruta and Samrat, for their encouragement, patience, buoyancy and good spirit during the editing of this volume. They have truly shared in its gestation, which was much longer than expected

Last but not the least, I am grateful to Gyan Publishing House, New Delhi for undertaking the publication of the book.

Sarthak Sengupta

List of Contributors

Dinesh Baishya, Department of Zoology, B. Barua College, Guwahati, Assam, 781 007

Indira Barua, Department of Anthropology, Dibrugarh University, Dibrugarh, Assam, 786 004

Dwipen Bezbaruah, Department of Anthropology, Gauhati University, Gopinath Bordoloi Nagar, Jalukbari, Guwahati, Assam, 781 014

Sapu Changkija, Department of Genetics and Plant Breeding, School of Agricultural Sciences and Rural Development, Nagaland University, Nagaland

Sanjita Chetia, Department of Home Science, Digboi Mahila Mahavidyalaya, Digboi, Assam

Sarit Kumar Choudhuri, Department of Anthropology, Rajib Gandhi University, Rono Hills, Doimukh, Itanagar, Arunachal Pradesh

Girin Das, District Research Officer, Diphu, Karbi Anglong, Assam

Sudakshina Das, Department of Zoology, D.H.S.K. College Dibrugarh,, Assam, 786 001

Fr K.M. Francis, Don Bosco School, Wokha, Nagaland.

Junu Mahanta, Department of English, D.D.R. College, Chabua, Dibrugarh, Assam

Lorho Mary Maheo, Department of Anthropology, United College, Lambung, Chandel, Manipur, 795 127

Birinchi Kumar Medhi, Department of Anthropology, Gauhati University, Gopinath Bordoloi Nagar, Jalukbari, Guwahati, Assam, 781 014

Sekh Rahim Mondal, Department of Anthropology, North Bengal University, Raja Rammohanpur, Darjeeling, North Bengal, 734 430

Sankar Kumar Roy, Department of Anthropology, Gauhati University, Gopinath Bordoloi Nagar, Jalukbari, Guwahati, Assam, 781 014

Mahaswetta Saikia, Department of Botany, University of Delhi, Delhi, 110 007

Sucheta Sen Choudhuri, Department of Anthropology, Rajib Gandhi University, Rono Hills, Doimukh, Itanagar, Arunachal Pradesh

Konsam Saratchandra Singh, Department of Anthropology, Manipur University, Canchipur, Imphal, Manipur, 795 003

Manish Sharma, Department of Economics, Government College, Bomdila, Arunachal Pradesh

1

Anthropology and the Study of Indigenous Knowledge –Perspective from North East India

Sekh Rahim Mondal

The subject of indigenous knowledge, natural resource management and development are the key issues of discussion in contemporary social science research. One of the major themes of "International Decade of Community and Development" during 1990's was to recognise the cultural diversity and indigenous knowledge system as alternative approach of development. The International Convention for Safeguarding of Intangible Cultural Heritage by UNESCO in 2003 also advocated the necessities of survival and validity of the world's living local, regional and national cultural heritage in the face of increasing globalisation and cultural homogenisation. The experts of cultural studies and organisations around the world called upon not only to document the indigenous knowledge system and intangible cultural heritage, but also encouraged for their preservation, protection, presentation and transmission for development of the indigenous communities.

The present chapter is a modest attempt to discuss the role of anthropology and anthropologists in documentation, protection and promotion of indigenous knowledge system. The chapter shall also highlight the role of indigenous knowledge and their sustainability in the contemporary changing world.

The chapter attempts to focus on the question of indigenous knowledge of the folk communities and their significance in development discourse with particular reference to North East India.

Indigenous People and Indigenous Knowledge

The term indigenous may be examined in different perspectives. In chronological sense, "indigenous" indicates earliest inhabitants if not autochthons. While in relational sense it indicate peoples who were under colonial dispensation and now occupy a poor and marginalised position in national societies. In normative sense, it covers people who feel rooted nests in their surroundings, entertain a custodial sense about their territory and resources, and bound together primarily through moral bindings and entertain a sense of reciprocity and mutuality reinforced by egalitarian ethos.

Etymologically the term indigenous carries with it several meanings, but anthropologically the concept attaches to an ethno-social and ethno-cultural entity. The term indigenous is unmanly equated with the tribal and folk communities, but considering historical connections and rootedness in the surroundings it also incorporates the other social categories, specially the peasants and marginal communities.

The ideas and practices of the indigenous communities to meet up their needs under specific environmental settings may be designated as indigenous knowledge, which they develop traditionally through life experience. The indigenous knowledge consists of the little traditions, which propagated, percolated, and transmitted orally from generation to generation. Actually, the age-old women as well as men of folk communities are the treasures of the indigenous knowledge system (ILO Convention 169 of 1989; Roy Burman, 2000).

Indigenous Knowledge and Cultural Heritage

Living in the realm of natural and social environments people create both tangible and intangible elements which help in promoting heritage formation that express the continuity of life in all its diversity. Culture and heritage manifest themselves not only in tangible form but also through intangible ideas and values.

The indigenous knowledge are the intangible cultural heritage of the folk communities which include ideas, voices, values, traditions, morality, oral history, folk life creativity, adaptability and distinctiveness of the people. These are manifested through dwelling, clothing, cooking, traditional skills, technology, ceremonies, manners, customs, performing arts, story telling, and so on.

The unique cultural heritage of the different parts of the world is the product of indigenous knowledge system of the communities living in diverse habitat of the globe; and which is always in the process of invention, diffusion, dissemination, accumulation, transformation and evolution. There is a popular saying that "Death of an old man and woman is equivalent to loss of a library". Indigenous knowledge system and intangible cultural heritage has been mostly presented and passed on to the present generation by the older generation in under developed region of the globe. In the face of the formidable market oriented forces of globalisation the voices of the indigenous people and their influences has been very weak and feeble. As a result, the local cultures and heritages are facing annihilation under emerging circumstances. Hence, the most urgent task is to affirm and agree that culture and civilisations do not clash rather they are dependent upon each other and can prosper in harmony and coexistence. The tangible heritage is the product of intangible knowledge and which is the creative force of humankind especially of indigenous communities, which needs to be explored and examined in the present juncture.

In recent times, environmental resource management and conservation of bio-diversity are the key issues of achieving sustainable development of the people of a particular place. The conservation and utilisation of natural resource depends on community management which is indeed dependant on their indigenous knowledge to manage the system. Discovery of indigenous knowledge of a region has a practical applicability not only for that region but also for other regions with necessary modifications. The indigenous knowledge system contains ample scope of formulating alternative development model of sustainable nature. The indigenous knowledge is the product of the folk communities, which is usually propagated in local conditions thus their validity and sustainability cannot be questioned (IGRMS, 1996; ICOM, 2004).

Anthropology and the Study of Indigenous Knowledge

In order to retain their relevance in the vast changing world, anthropologists have started to play a new role in the protection of cultural diversity and indigenous knowledge system, which go hand in hand. The traditional knowledge bases of the communities of the world over are now being threatened and eroded by the growing tide of technologies, modernisation and homogenisation of the planet. Development that has taken the form of mega projects destroys the habitats of the indigenous communities along with the bio-diversity of their habitat. Such destruction may drag humankind particularly the indigenous communities towards gradual extinction. Under such a changing context, there is an urgent need of documentation, protection and promotion of traditional heritages and indigenous knowledge systems.

In contemporary times, the post-modern thrust in anthropology has compelled them to think about discourse analysis in the context of development and progress of the humankind. The discourse analysis starts with "deconstruction" of the concept of development. The discourses of development as constructed by the West are not only dominant but very biased as they carried with themselves the hegemonic philosophy and power of their source. The relation between knowledge and power in respect to ideology of progress is very implicit in the context of development as put forwarded by the West. The Western discourse of development is closely associated with materialism and consumerism, which is entirely alien to the life ways of the folk and indigenous communities. Thus, the local knowledge and discourse, which are historically derived over centuries, adopted to local environment and embedded in the entire complex of social relations and cultural practices, are considered to be alien to dominant western discourse of development. Therefore, the local or alternative discourse as against dominant western discourse has much greater significance in development process of the indigenous societies.

The Anthropologists are now been realised that the protection of indigenous knowledge and cultural diversity will come from the recognition of cultural plurality and complexity, which should coexist with harmony and consensus. The elements of culture like that of knowledge, language, and practices can not be viewed and exhibited from the perspective of domination and subordination rather they should be considered as unique and exclusive. Therefore, attention must be paid to analyse and interpret them in the context of nature and nature specific to temporal and spatial dimensions.

Anthropology has long been considered as a discipline of exploring, analysing and exhibiting both tangible and intangible cultural elements, traits and trait complexes of the indigenous communities. They considered being the experts of cultural studies by virtue of their intensive long-term fieldwork among the indigenous communities. Their field work technique of participant observation and holistic approach of understanding the life ways of folk communities have much potential to explore and examine the knowledge base of such people whom they studied intensively.

Anthropologists today have to play a new role in exhibiting, protecting and promoting indigenous knowledge system to retain the cultural diversity against hegemonic forces of cultural homogenisation and unauthorised extraction of cultural resources for market interest of the West. In order to fulfill this role, the contemporary anthropologists are more relying upon *emic* and participatory approach of study for helping the indigenous communities to codify, clarify, analyse, maintain and communicate the cultural data in their own languages and dialects. They also help the people to explore and strengthen the indigenous knowledge systems, customs, myths and rituals to live in harmony within their habitat and environment. They are also concerned with the exploration of valuable and dormant cultural elements and to replenish them to sustain the indigenous heritages for well being of the mankind as a whole. The knowledge systems, habits and cultural landscapes of the indigenous communities are no doubt living but struggling to survive under changing global atmosphere. Under such a context, considering the demand of the situation, anthropologists must collaborate with the communities in their cultural recuperation and self-determination. With this changing role, anthropologists no longer are treated by the communities as data hungry persons, but as partners in the struggle for their restitution, preservation and promotion of cultural heritages. Contemporary anthropologists must extend their horizon of study not only to examine the cultural attributes and objects of the communities and their knowledge bases, those create such attributes and objects. For doing so, they must engage themselves in cross-cultural studies with objective of developing channels for intra-cultural and inter-cultural transfer of knowledge and technology and to recognise as well as combat the problems, which endanger such communities with cultural and biological extinction. This may be considered as a strategy of social care and concern for the indigenous people (Lewellen, 2002; Chaudhury, 1982; Vidyarthi, 1986).

Indigenous Knowledge and the North East India

The North East India is, often referred as Seven Sisters or rainbows coalitions, which comprise Seven States viz. Assam, Manipur, Meghalaya, Nagaland, Mizoram, Tripura and Arunachal Pradesh. The States of North East India are located at the foothills of the Himalayas in which we find mountainous terrains, plateaus and plains criss-crossed by rivers and rivulets. The region is bestowed with rich natural resources of land, water, vegetation and animals. It is well known for its climatic, floral and faunal diversities.

The North East region of India is the home of a large number of diverse and colourful ethnic groups. The ethnic groups of this region are usually referred as Indo –Mongoloids, and particularly known as *Kiratas* (non-Aryan origin). More than 276 distinct ethnic groups who are indigenous or early settlers if not autochthones inhabit the region. Considering the indigenous ethnic stocks, the North East India represents the highest diversity of ethno-cultural groups featuring a mosaic of cultural and linguistic varieties with distinctive identities.

By living with the rich, diverse and unique natural surroundings traditionally, the people of North East India perceived and managed the environment resources of their respective habitats to fulfill the basic needs. They meet their needs through a long tradition of carefully managing natural resources. The land, the vegetation, the animal and the other natural resources are used and managed by the people on their perception of man-environment relation and to which their indigenous knowledge support system are indeed playing a very significant role.

The cultural beliefs and practices of the indigenous peoples of this region have in fact contributed a lot to biological diversity and environmental protection. Their environment within which they live in supports all their food, clothing, shelter, medicine and other requirements. The principle of co-existence between natural environment and human being is a unique phenomenon of this region and which is possible due to knowledge base of the indigenous communities, which they developed out of experience in life system. The traditional utilisation of diverse environmental resources by indigenous communities in North East region not only reflects a diverse resource use pattern but also a wise way of maintaining and sustaining the regions rich bio-diversity in the eco-system. The life ways of the peoples of this region has been operating under indigenous system for centuries. However, in recent time there are several forces of change in indigenous practices and technologies, which have several consequences both to environmental resources as well as to peoples of North East region. Considering such an emerging problem there is an urgent need to identify, document and study of indigenous knowledge systems and practices of the region through proper research (Aier and Changkija, 2003; Dubey, 1978; Sahu, 2002; Subba and Ghosh, 2003).

Epilogue

Of late, it has been realised that knowledge system of the indigenous communities and their cultural heritage has much potentials for development as an alternative model against the dominant western one. Since the indigenous knowledge systems and ideas are changing very fast in the era of globalisation, there is an urgent need for their documentation, preservation and promotion for the well-being of both indigenous and non-indigenous communities. Anthropology being the holistic science of man has to play a very crucial role to contribute towards exploration, documentation and education of such vanishing cultural resources.

Anthropologists of 21st century are very much concerned with the protection of the validity of cultural diversities and pluralities of human articulation. As such Anthropologists of today are not only concerned with the indigenous societies representing vanishing cultures, but of the vital and relevant patterns of those cultures. Since the pattern of culture is deeply embedded in traditional knowledge systems, hence they realised the need of its revitalisation. Contemporary anthropological studies are more concerned with cultural processes of the indigenous groups rather than with the products and with the context, ethics and implications of such processes.

Many anthropologists all over the world have now realised the significance of cultural diversities against the cultural uniformities as set up by the New World Order through the process of globalisation. In this context, they are much concerned with the exploration and documentation of traditional knowledge systems of the indigenous communities. For the study of knowledge, resources of the indigenous group's anthropologists continue their core business of data collection from the field situation and interpret their field data from the perspectives of the people for necessary documentation, preservation and education. The collection, documentation and interpretation of indigenous knowledge system, not only help in understanding the cultural identities of diverse groups but also contribute to promote harmony, peace and prosperity in diversity.

Diverse ethnic, social and cultural groups inhabit the North East Region of India; each of them has their own traditional knowledge system and survival strategy based on resource available in the respective habitat. The traditional utilisation of environmental resources by indigenous communities of North East region not only reflects their indigenous knowledge system or diverse resource use pattern but also highlight the ways of maintaining and sustaining the bio-diversity of the place. The discovery and study of indigenous knowledge and practices in relation to environmental resource management has a great practical applicability as these have tremendous potential for achieving sustainable development of this region.

References

Aier, A and S. Changkija., 2003, "Indigenous Knowledge and Management of Natural Resources", in T.B. Subba and G.C. Ghosh (Eds) : *The Anthropology of North East India.* New Delhi: Orient Longman Pvt. Ltd.

Choudhury, B., 1982, *Tribal Development in India.* New Delhi: Inter India Publications.

Dubey, S.M., 1978, *North East India: A Sociological Study.* New Delhi: Concept Publishing Company.

ICOM, 2004, *Museum and Intangible Heritage.* Korea : ICOM Seoul Conference.

Indira Gandhi Rastriya Manav Sangrahalaya., 1996, *On National Museum of Man.* Bhopal: Indira Gandhi Rastriya Manav Sangrahalaya.

Lewellen, T.C., 2002, *The Anthropology of Globalisation: Cultural Anthropology Enters the 21st Century.* London: Bergin and Garvey.

Roy Burman, B.K., 2000, *Indigenous and Tribal Peoples of Eastern India and Bangladesh: Indigenisation and Alternative Designs of Globalisation.* Kolkata : Department of Anthropology. Calcutta University.

Sahu, C., 2002, *Tribes of North East India: An Ethnographic Profile.* New Delhi: Sarup and Sons.

Subba, T.B. and G.C. Ghosh., 2003, *The Anthropology of North East India: A Text Book.* New Delhi: Orient Longman Pvt. Ltd.

Vidyarthi, L.P., 1986, *Tribal Development and Its Administration,* New Delhi: Concept Publishing Company.

2

Indigenous Knowledge of Sustainable Mountain Farming System Practices in North East India

Sapu Changkija

Geographically the North East India consisting of seven States is the meeting point of historical-ecological peripheries of the South, Southeast, East and Central Asia. The region covers the mountains of eastern Himalayas and the Patkai range. Physically the region contains the upland watersheds of major rivers systems in the Asian continental region, including the Brahmaputra, Barak and Irrawaddy. The climatic condition ranges from wet-tropical in the plains, sub-tropical in the middle and temperate in the high hills of monsoon with excessive rainfall. The vegetation ranges from wet-tropical forest to cool temperate alpine forests of evergreen and deciduous types. All the seven States border on international boundaries. It has 1350 km. long border with China in the north, 900 km. long border with Bangladesh in the Southeast, and a 2350 km. long border with Myanmar in the east. However, with the rest of the Indian union, the region is linked only through the State of Assam by a narrow strip of land measuring 38 kms connecting it with West Bengal (Borthakur, 1992). This region is bestowed with rich natural resources of land and water with its rich floral and faunal diversity, land use patterns, agricultural practices and traditional knowledge base. Judicious exploitation of these resources could have brought prosperity to the region as the world has recognised it as one of the 18th hot spots of mega bio-diversity due to its species richness and high level of endemism. The region also consists of the highest diversity of ethno-cultural groups featuring a mosaic of cultural, linguistic variations with distinctive identities. More than 276 indigenous ethnic groups (Singh, 1999) inhabit this region. Many of the indigenous tribal groups have their counterparts across the international boundary in Tibet, Yunnan province of China, Thailand, Laos, Cambodia, Myanmar and Chittagong hill tracts of Bangladesh (Anonymous, 1997).

Indigenous knowledge is often considered as informal knowledge that exists in local societies in comparison with formal knowledge developed by universities and research institutions of modern society (Shingji, 1995). The indigenous knowledge systems of a local society cover a wide range of its member perceptions of universal phenomena occurring in their immediate environment and practices on every aspect of social, economic and cultural activities taking place within the society. It is the product of centuries of experiences acquired and developed in a spectrum of information, skills and technology. Over a period of several hundred years, farmers themselves have tested, implemented, evaluated, modified and developed practice in the system of agriculture, soil conservation and fertility management, irrigation, livestock management, forest management, and so on for their sustenance. It plays very important role in developing self-sufficiency and self-determination, strengthening the people's participation and sustainability. In many instances, indigenous knowledge will be a blend of locally rooted and exogenous knowledge crafted to suit local situations. Some of the indigenous knowledge practices of the hill tribes in the region with regard to agricultural systems are highlighted in brief as follows:

Soil Conservation and Fertility Management Practices

Conservation and management of soil fertility is the most basic and crucial issue to any agricultural community. Erosion of soil surface leading to the topsoil removal, nutrient loss and rapid run-off, is the major concern of the farmers especially in this region. Soil is the single most important non-renewable resource for people's food and livelihood security in mountain area. Virtually all agriculture workers agree that poor soil fertility is one of the major constraints facing farmers in the mountains but there has been no concerted effort to characterise the soils. Studies on indigenous fertility management indicate that farmers are not managing their land as well as they might. In the long history of struggle for survival and for getting enough food, the people in the region have evolved number of indigenous practices, which improved soil conservation and fertility management. Agricultural scientists have been slow to understand the complexity of traditional soil fertility management and consequently have been unable to improve substantially traditional management systems (Carson, 1992).

The hills tribes of the North East India are marginal farmers of sloping lands which face the major problem run-off of top soil due to heavy rainfall and thereby loss of fertility. In order to reduce the run-off of topsoil, counter such problems and other related problems they practice many excellent indigenous technologies on soil conservation and soil fertility management, such as:

- Minimum tillage of the soil (*Jhuming* / Shifting cultivation is a sustainable and minimum tillage farming system).
- Watershed management with integration of animal husbandry (*Zabo* farming system).
- Use of nitrogen fixing plant species in shifting cultivation (*Alder* base farming system).
- Contour tillage.
- Soil traps and barriers of horizontal rows on the slope lands at regular intervals.
- Soil traps of drop structures.
- Crop rotation.
- Growing cover crops on the slope land to conserve the soil.
- Bench terrace farming system (water and soil management farming system).
- Constructions of terrace riser slicing.
- Construction of soil erosion barriers.

- Construction of diversion ditches.
- Construction of water harvesting pond.
- Composting and mulching.
- Spreading ashes.
- Spreading litters collected from the forests.
- Spreading of animal waste.
- *In-situ* manuring.
- Grass strips plantation.
- Use of legumes for soil re-acclimatisation.
- Use of ashes.
- Use of Farm Yard Manure (FYM).
- Use of green manure.
- Use of residual maters of households.
- Use of salt as weedicides.
- Plantation of deep-rooted plant species (to hold the land/ soil in the critical slopes) etc.

Indigenous Farming Practices in the Region

Indigenous farming system practices are a primary source of sustenance for the mountain populations in the region. Because of population pressure, degradation of slope lands, low productivity, inadequate access to appropriate technology, etc., agriculture is being stretched beyond their tolerable limits to meet the growing demands of food and other products of day-to-day needs. Generally, agriculture in the mountain systems is an integral land based activity and management of cropping, animal husbandry, horticulture, forestry, soil conservation, and their linkages and support systems. Many technological interventions, research and developmental initiatives have been carried out towards maximising production – promoting external inputs in the mountain farming systems, which succeeded only partially, remaining limited geographically to more arable areas. Due to hilly terrain and undulating topography, the scope for the use of modern machinery in this region is limited. Small land holding and lack of financial sources have restricted the choice of the farmers to invest more on critical inputs in order to get higher yields. Further, the systems are indigenously designed and modified to meet the various needs of the rural farmers for their livelihood and which are supported by the forest eco-systems. Cultivation of the upland and hill slopes is practiced, either through some conservation measures or directly on the slopes. Some of the existing systems are discussed as follows:

Shifting Cultivation

The shifting cultivation is a form of low-input agriculture and fallow management is common in North East India particularly in paddy, taro, maize, legumes, cucurbits and, cassava-based system. It is also commonly referred to as Swidden or *Jhum* cultivation. This is a sustainable practice in sparsely populated areas keeping long duration of fallow. It is the most widespread type of cropping system and is directly supported by the forest eco-system. Shifting cultivation system is a reflection of man-environment relationship in the tropical mountain region, which is evolved along with the issue of forest management. Otherwise, this system is characterised by highly diversified cropping pattern thereby meeting the peoples' needs for food, medicine and aromatics, etc., besides maintaining the germ plasm of the indigenous crop varieties. It has been in use for centuries and remains a major land use practice, which provides a basis for subsistence farming maintenance of cultural values and social stability for the people living in low population densities. In the mountain tribal communities of the region, shifting cultivation is a way of life and all elements of their social life are geared to, and integrated into the continued operation of their culture. In this system, the jungle is cut and burned and food crops are then planted using minimum tillage practices with crop rotation system. This helps in weed control in the first three months enabling crops to grow quickly, retain soil moisture and obtain maximum nutrients available in the soil by mix cropping.

Alder Based Shifting Cultivation

The Naga tribe, particularly Angami, Konyak and Sema Naga practice the "Alder tree based" shifting cultivation as an indigenous innovation of soil fertility management. The farmers are specialised and have perfected to an excellent cultivation system in which they incorporate the natural nitrogen fixing plant *Alnus nepalensis* (called Alder trees). This system consists of the proper use of forestland maintenance of natural trees in the *jhum* fields to manage the soil fertility. It has been found that the Alder based shifting cultivation system allows the soil to regenerate faster and the *jhum* cycle can be managed at a four years cycle with two years of cropping followed by two or more years fallow. It also greatly reduces the labour input in the clearing of fallows. This system is identified as one of the most promising bio-physically workable and socially acceptable indigenously innovated adoption towards fallow management (Changkija *et al.*, 1998). In this system, the naturally grown Alder trees are cut or pollarded at a height of about two meters from the ground to obtain a head of shoots, which are nurtured during the *jhum* period. New sapling is also planted and is left to mature during the fallow period to be pollarded at the next *jhum* cycle. The branches so cut are used or sold as fuel wood.

Wet Terraced Paddy Cultivation

This type of cultivation system is practiced in the hill slopes wherever sufficient water is available. These are not rain-fed but irrigated using local skills. Terraces are cut into the slopes, flooded carefully using bamboo, and local materials as water conduits. This irrigated terraced cultivation types are practiced by the Angami, Zeliangrong, and Chakesang of Nagaland; Apatani and Nishis in Arunachal Pradesh and Khasi in Meghalaya. In this type of cultivation, suitable terraces are located and short-term fish farming in combination with paddy is practiced during the monsoon.

Apatani System of Water Management

In the Apatani system of wet terraced cultivation, they maintain a carefully designed irrigation system. In this system, each stream is tapped soon after it emerges from the forest and reaches a gully wide enough to accommodate a series of terraces. A short distance from the terraces occurs the first diversion from the stream but usually only a little water is deflected here. The stream continues on its course while the feeder channel branching off at an angle leads water alongside the series of terraces. So that by blocking or opening the connecting duct any field can be flooded or drained as required. Similar cultivation is also found in Changki and Medzephima Valleys in Nagaland, Nongpoh area in Meghalaya, and Champai Valley in Mizoram.

Bamboo Drip Irrigation

The Jaintias of Meghalaya commonly practices this system of water management. It is also a low cost irrigation system using locally available materials like bamboo. The bamboo ducts are laid at an elevated height supported by bamboo or wooden props. Such bamboo water lines are taken even over very long distances for irrigation or watering the farmland. Such water management practice prevents water percolation in the water scarce area. It is a unique example of efficient management of available scarce water and reflects the foresightedness of the tribal farmers.

Zabo Farming System

Zabo is a kind of mix farming system, which is traditionally practiced in Phek district of Nagaland. It is a combination of forestry, agriculture, livestock rearing and fishery with well-founded soil and water conservation basis. It envisages proper utilisation of rainwater and maintenance of soil fertility using organic sources of crop nutrition and biomass accumulation.

Home / Kitchen Garden

Home or kitchen gardens work as indigenous soil fertility management ways at small scale and is being practiced by the farmers in the mountains. This system is low labour consuming, which has proven to be sustainable and adaptable under diverse environmental conditions. This is known to complement shifting agriculture and animal husbandry practices utilising land and other resources extremely efficiently in mountain areas. In the system farmers manage, a simple, small farm in homestead is where various crops, medicinal herbs, flower, and fodder can be grown and become significant commercial enterprises for supplying high value goods to the market. It is one of the most intensively cultivated agro-ecosystems. In this a mixture of many plant species are planted, mainly fruit trees, root crops, seasonal vegetables, medicinal and ornamental plants as both a repository and testing site for uncommon species. This also become a source of subsistence and cash incomes. A total of 128 number of various plant species are listed, which are grown in the home garden in Nagaland (Changkija, 1992). Many opportunities are made available to greatly increase production, primarily because of the proximity of the kitchen garden to the homestead. Waste drainage water from the kitchen can be used to start seedling or irrigate annual crops. Ashes and sweeps from the households and domestic animals bedding are normally spread in the garden and it does enrich the soil around the homestead. Given the above, it is not surprising that the kitchen garden, though small in total area, is an important part of the overall production system and has successfully been used as an entry point into the enhanced productivity of the farming system.

Agro Forestry

Agro forestry is the deliberate growth and management of trees along with agricultural crops and or livestock. It is a system that is ecologically, socially and economically sustainable. Agriculture with a wide diversity of plant species is a solution which seems more suitable for humid tropical and sub tropical region in the North East India. Agro forestry in the region has evolved over a century and is very diverse and complex. Today, as the condition changes, farmers continue to innovate, experiment and improve the systems. To meet their needs of fodder and fuel wood, fibers, and cash, farmers integrate agricultural crops, trees and livestock in these farming systems. This integration has resulted in a wide diversity of traditional agro forestry system. Most of these systems are well suited to the local agro-ecological conditions, the specific subsistence and cash needs of farmers, their social and cultural context and the environmental conservation needs.

The higher altitude or densely populated areas of Arunachal Pradesh, Nagaland, Sikkim have developed practices to integrate their farming systems with adjoining forests to graze their yaks, *mithuns*, cattle, goats and sheep in the forests, or develop forests / gardens to meet their subsistence and cash needs. In the lower altitudes, in the foothills and areas adjoining the plains, agro forestry of very specific trees that take long time to produce yield (e.g., coconut, areca-nut, rubber, thatching-palm, mango, jack-fruit, litchi, betel-vine, black-pepper, coffee etc.), along with short term crop combinations are also developed.

In the middle hills of the region, most settlements with higher population develop the agro forestry practices. Their emphasis is on growing local needs such as bamboo, constructional wood, fuel wood, thatching-palm, broomstick, fruits tree, along with the various crops for their sustenance. Agro forestry systems, particularly in high population and fuel-wood deficit areas, can serve buffer zones to mitigate the degradation of natural and plantation forests.

Table 2.1: Blending Indigenous and Exogenous Knowledge in Mountain Farming

Indigenous practice	*Indigenous practice blended with exogenous knowledge*	*Practiced by the ethnic group*
1. Carry biomass the forest and mulch or burn it on field.	Promote trees and crops growing on farm for biomass production	Chakesang, Ao, Tangkhul, Mao, Jaintia, Khasi.
2. Burn plant residues in the farm and distribute the ashes.	Reduce burning on farm; incorporate at least half of the unburned residues into the soil.	Angami, Ao, Sema, Lotha, Rengma, Mao, Konyaks, Garo, Kachari.
3. Build walls from dry branches, shrubs and bamboo	Combine wall with contour ditch uphill from wall. Strengthen wall with live hedge rows.	Ao, Lotha, Rengma, Konyak, Garo, Nishi, Adi, Wancho.
4. Integrate trees into fields.	Improve planting patterns of existing practice.	Angami, Mao, Khasi, Mishing, Adi, Nishi, Konyak, Wancho, Ao, Jaintia, Karbi.
5. Build rock terraces.	Strengthen terraces and control soil erosion	Angami, Chakesang, Mao, Monpa.

Indigenous practice	*Indigenous practice blended with exogenous knowledge*	*Practiced by the ethnic group*
6. Build log or bamboo terraces.	Strengthen terraces, control soil erosion and fertilise the soil by its decomposition.	Mizo, Ao, Karbi, Kachari, Lotha, Sangtam, Konyak.
7. Build terraces from the unburned twigs and biomass.	Strengthen the terrace, control soil erosion and fertilise the soil by its decomposition.	Chakesang, Sema, Ao, Lotha, Konyak, Kuki, Nishi, Adi.
8. Weeds/green biomass kept on the surface or rocks and top of the tree stumps without contact with the soil.	Recycling biomass by exposing to dryness and decomposed to fertilise the soil. It also controls the growth of coppices in the stumps.	Ao, Lotha, Rengma, Mizo, Konyak, Garo, Kachari, Adi, Nishi, Khiamungan Yimchunger.
9. Banana, plantains and leaves use in contour lines and nursery for growing seedlings.	Cooling and moistening of the soil during dry seasons.	Chakesang, Angami, Ao, Lotha, Sangtam, Konyak, Garo, Karbi, Kachari, Mishing.
10. Bamboo used in channeling water and for water tripling irrigation.	An efficient irrigation system	Jaintia, Khasi, Garo, Mizo, Angami, Ao, Lotha, Mao, Tangkhul.

Farmers have to store their products firstly for seeds and secondly for consumption and sale of the marketable surplus. The indigenous practices followed by the farmers of the region for storing of paddy are almost similar in the region although there are some variations in minor details. The most common method of storing paddy for consumption or sale is to have to separate storehouse for each family/household with raised wooden or bamboo platform (floor). The storehouse has two floors; the first one is like a platform and there is an upper higher floor for storing paddy. A smooth flat wooden plate or a tin shed is fitted to each supporting pole of the storehouse so that the rats cannot climb up crossing the horizontal plate. The ladder that is used for going up to the stores is not attached to the platform. A separately kept ladder is used at the time of climbing only, thus ensuring that the rats do not climb up to the higher platform through the ladder. Farmers store un-husked paddy after threshing and sometimes they apply some plants such as *Letsea citrata, Artimesea vulgaris* etc., or those plant extracts as insecticide. Storing paddy for future seeds is done in a different manner and usually kept in warm places in a bamboo woven container. The seeds are kept in especially made bamboo cylinder or in cylinder made of *Luffa cylindrical* or in pumpkin cylinders.

Pest Control

Traditional pest control practices were fine-tuned to the tribal environment using traditional systems such as the settled, poly-cultural home-gardens and fallow shifting cultivation. Such low-input farming systems are ecologically and culturally sustainable and they have succeeded in keeping pest problems to a minimum. When problems arise, such as attacks by rats, locust and various insects, locally available materials and knowledge were used to reduce losses. These traditional pest control practices formed an important component of mountain farming systems, contributing to their flexibility, productivity and sustainability. Historically, post harvest pests are not a problem among the tribal, as most produce is consumed locally soon after harvesting. Small amounts of processed foods are adequately stored by means of traditional indigenous technique, in specifically made containers in the smoked-filled kitchen an environment that is not favourable for pests. Vertebrates such as rats, squirrels, birds and insects like locust, aphids, weevil, bugs, caterpillars, etc., cause the major pest problems in the region. To control the pest, farmers use various techniques such as traps, barriers and wrapping, hand-picking, spreading of some particular plant crushed, fumigation by the plant extracts, burning, scanning devices, smoking, and introduction of insects or vertebrates. The tribals also eat some insects such as locust, weevil and some particular bugs, ants, caterpillars and spiders.

PH Control

Indigenous innovation of the hill farmers especially in Nagaland is the use of lime and salt as pesticide and weedicide. This method is widely practiced in Mokokchung district of Nagaland by the Ao Naga tribes. Depending upon the problems in the farm, the farmer soak either lime or salt in water and sprinkled on the soil, which kills the weeds as well as certain pests. On farmer's information, the crop yield is higher from fields where salt or lime is used. This is because both the agents are alkaline which reduces the high acidity PH of the soil.

Discussion

The challenges that mountain traditional societies in the region are facing in the transformation from subsistence economy to a market oriented ones are varied, complex, and difficult. Modern external interventions, which are negatively effecting mountain communities, are being implemented at great speed without regard for tribal traditional systems and natural resources management system in the region, which can be so diverse from one place and community to the other. There is also a tremendous pressure of socio-economic change and with this the ecological knowledge and cultural traditions, which have been continuously developed and transferred from generation to generation, are beginning to be lost. It is time to realise that traditional knowledge and management systems are as important as the need to introduce modern innovative approaches to sustainable development and management of natural resources in order to sustain the livelihood of traditional societies in this region. The understanding of indigenous knowledge and practices in relation to bio-diversity resource management is one of the key issues for achieving sustainable development of this region as the production system in this region has been operating under indigenous systems for centuries, which is being continued. Some of the rational indigenous technologies need preservation without which they tend to fade away gradually and their revival in the future become impossible. They are not only of value for the culture from which they evolve but also for the scientists and planners striving to improve conditions in rural societies (Warren, 1990).

No doubt, not all indigenous knowledge systems and practices may be scientific or sustainable. Nevertheless, with necessary technical and scientific inputs, they contain ample scope for formulating development alternatives with minimum costs. Therefore, it would be worthwhile to examine and encourage building upon the existing indigenous systems in planning for sustainable development of the hilly areas in this region.

The agricultural systems of the hill areas of the region have not been studied adequately. As innovation that promotes local resource management attracts more attention on alternative, regenerative options are needed for the rehabilitation of irrigated support lands and better management of natural resources (Partap and Watson, 1994). The alternative technological options are also expected to open up income opportunities for poorer mountain farmer groups. However, these technical improvements will be accepted only when they can lead to increased productivity and profitability. There are however a number of agricultural systems which with proper management and encouragement will have tremendous potential for intensification without disturbing the soil or forest ecology.

References

Anonymous, 1997. "North East of India: A Report". *The North East Voice*, Vol. No. 5.

Borthakur, D.N., 1992, *Agriculture of the North East Reegion*. Guwahati: Bee Cee Prakashan.

Carson, B., 1992, *The Land, the Farmer, and the Future*. ICIMOD Occasional Paper No. 21. Kathmandu : ICIMOD.

Changkija, S.; A. Yaden and A. Aier, 1998, "Case Study on Traditional Indigenous Farming System Practices Based on Alder Trees (*Alnus nepalensis*) by the Naga Tribes of Nagaland, India", in *Proceedings in Search of Sustainability and Ecological Security in the Eastern Hills of India*". Lumami: Nagaland University.

Partap, T and H.R. Watson, 1994, *Sloping Agricultural Land Technology (SALT), A Regenerative Option for Sustainable Mountain Farming*. ICIMOD Occasional Paper. Kathmandu : ICIMOD.

Shingji, P., 1995, "Sustainable Livelihood for Mountain Communities: Traditionand Transition in Natural Resource Management", *IPS Workshop to Development Projections on Resource Management and Sustainable Livelihood for Traditional Societies in South and Central Asia.* 10-14 September 1995.

Singh, K.S., 1999, "Face to Face". *Grassroots Options*, (interview) Monsoon issue, Shillong.

Warren, D.M., 1990, "Indigenous Knowledge and Development". *Background Paper for Seminar Session on Sociology, Natural Resources Management and Agri- development.* The World Bank, December 3, 1990.

3

Indigenous Knowledge and the Right to Work for Development–A Gendered Perspective

Sucheta Sen Choudhuri

The closeness between women and indigenous knowledge: A study report says "...... in Manipur we had entire range of textile technology and development process can be noticed very well since all stages of technology is visibly present. That is the reason the women of Manipur, irrespective of groups can give varieties of textile designs, what we have done so far was not a positive development but conveniently killed some aspects of scientific knowledge" (Ghosh and Ghosh, 1997). Ghosh and Ghosh (*ibid,* 121-152) had reached to such conclusion during the study on contribution of women of Manipur in sericulture. A detailed study is done on the life cycle of silk worms, production of cocoons, entire ecological background of silk production, and technological aspects of it. Now I am sharing one of my very thought provoking experience. I was working in an Assamese village in the district Kamrup, Assam. One morning in the kitchen of an Assamese family, I found that the aged father is taking full-grown dead silk worms from boiled cocoons and daughter at home is taking preparation for cooking of these worms. It was altogether a new sight for me. Further, to fulfill my enquiry they showed me the household kitchen garden where they cultivate these worms and cocoons for weaving. Lastly, she showed me *Mekhela Chaadar* (silk) and wrapper (*Endi Chaadar)*, along with cotton made weaving products of towel *(Gamocha)*, bed covers. I had seen varieties of productions of home at that village as I was working on the project related to women. In addition, in this village for the first time I came to know one fact that even today weaving is considered as one of the important qualifications for women during marriage in rural Assam.

I experienced the same in the Bodo villages of Kokrajhar, Nalbari and Darrang districts of Assam where women were more involved in the production of cotton weaving and their wisdom to promote it through cooperative system. It will not be out of context to mention another cultural trait of weaving, which was followed during the Bodo movement. Precisely, this is related to that one cultural trait of weaving revived during the Bodo movement. In medieval period, the Bodo warriors used to put on a cotton waist belt, which was believed protect the person from any misfortune. This belt was a special one. The custom of making this belt was that the mother, wife, or sister of the warrior would weave the belt within a night so silently that nobody will know it. Any kind of deviation from this custom was considered as the misfortune for the person. This custom was revived during the Bodo movement in a new form when girls in villages weave *Aronai* for the underground activists not informing any body else and presented these cloths to the activists through some simple rituals at *Bathousal* (alter of village deity). Such incident proves the closeness of customs of weaving to the society.

In the Wancho village of Tirap district, Arunachal Pradesh, I had experienced deep knowledge of women on technology of weaving and different stages of development as well as their closeness with nature. The women in village could make their loin looms of different sises by themselves. Different parts of loin looms are made from bamboo and wood. I cannot forget one incidence of Longding, Tirap district of Arunachal Pradesh. I was requesting a Wancho woman to show the spindle in which she spins cotton to make yarn. At first, she was not comfortable as she was unable to show it to me. Because she wanted to show me, something, which is available in the market and more over any such instrument, was not there in her possession. However, due to my repeated requests she sat to make one such instrument for me. She collected one 10-12 inch long bamboo stick of quarter inch diameter, and an orange. She had fitted the orange nearer to the lower end of the stick, started spinning cotton, and had produced yarn. I was astonished seeing her knowledge because I myself understood the fact since I have studied science. Precisely, what I understood was she had made a balance between weight and motion to make instrument in action. Next morning she presented me one such instrument replacing the orange with an unknown round shaped hard-coated seed.

In the Wancho villages of Zedua and Senua, I saw age-old cloths of women are made of creepers' fibre, which is not used nowadays. During winter it is a common scene in these villages, where old ladies dried cotton seeds on the roof or extended platforms, which are collected by family members from cultivable fields. Similarly, you may see the Wancho women are making grass necklaces when they are working at cultivable lands. These grass necklaces really served purpose of beautification or was part of dress to cover upper body.

Quite important is the knowledge of making natural dyes. Almost every community of Arunachal Pradesh developed technologies to prepare natural dyes. Differences in colours are also noticed and may be for that reason these colours became identity markers for communities. Moreover, the strength of knowledge in it is shadowed.

Social History of Weaving and Women in North East India

Any ethnographic writings mention women as the main occupants of weaving (Ghosh and Ghosh, 1997; Roy, 1979; Dai, 2002; Elwin, 1975). In Manipur, "every woman is an artisan and every home is a production centre of handlooms" (Roy, 1979). Linguistically, at least, several thousand vocabularies can be coined on woven staffs, looms, and different parts of looms.

Roy (1979) has given local names of tools used in weaving in different communities in Manipur as summarised in Table 3.1.

This table is only introducing us with names of machines. Roy (*ibid*) describes the structures of these machines along

Table 3.1. Local Names of Tools

Local names of tools in different communities						*English* equivalent
Meitei	*Kabuis*	*Hmars*	*Paiteis*	*Kukis*	*Tangkhuls*	
Kapteng	-	Heraat	Helhot	Pathkuam	-	Ginning Machine
Hutri	-	Patsai	Patphel	Patsai	-	Grading Machine
Maiyot	Mui	Hmuithal	Muitung	Hmuthal	-	Spinning Machine
Masha	Jak	Sutham	Suttam	Patlam	-	Winding Machine
Langtham	Langtham	-	-	-	-	Twisting Machine
Tareng	Tareng	Hmui	Mui	Hmui	Tareng	Spinning Wheel

Source: Roy, 1979:18

with functions. She *(ibid*: 14) has documented procedures of making suitable yarns for weaving. These are Ginning, Grading, Spinning, Winding, Twisting, Dyeing, Sising, and Bleaching etc.

Most of the communities have their own customs, beliefs, and folklore related to weaving and origin of weaving. In these stories, women were the characters. The "Tangkhuls discourage their girls from marrying with men of village where weaving is not practiced" (Roy, 1979). The Wancho women prepares natural dye silently, because they believe that shades of manufactured colour will be improper if any body outside home knows, or see it. In Manipur societies, crafts are considered as sacred duty (Roy, 1979).

Weaving is not a class less occupation in every tribal society. In the Wancho community, weaving was a job for women of chiefs' family and clans. Women of chiefs' family and clans usually did not go to cultivable field like women of commoners' clans. It does not mean that women of commoners' clans did not know weaving. They learnt it in their childhood from senior women because women of chiefs' clans were married to families of commoners' clans. Therefore, in any case it was a known craft for women but was more practiced by the women of chiefs' clans' family background. There are restrictions in using of motifs. Shape, size of motifs differ from chiefs' clans to commoners' clans (Choudhury, 2002). The Naga shawl manifests social status. Not all members of the community are entitled to all designs. The beauties of motifs and colour combinations are not considered as art only. This may be the reason of non-availability of these products in markets earlier. Women as producer could not enjoy freedom in using their knowledge to earn surplus. Though Roy (*op. cit*: 22) mentions, "The greatest advantage of these (Back Strap or Loin Looms) is that an unlimited range of varieties of designs can be produced. It is possible not only to weave short-width, but also to get well-designed heavy and compact textured fabrics in these looms. These advantages are mainly responsible for continued existence of this crude and outmoded looms in the face of competitions with other hand looms" (Roy, *op.cit*).

Art or Technology: A Phase of Confusion

The art in weaving, attracted more attention of the western and Indian scholars, to write on this where the technological innovations within it remained as an ignored area. Elwin (1988) criticised such attitudes of explorers, who were dominated by their own thought process and distinguished the western scientific knowledge with indigenous knowledge system. Such attitudes caused a great harm to the body of scientific knowledge of non-European communities. It remained an unwritten body of knowledge. Lacking in systematic recording to describe what it is, how it does, how it does it, and different phases of development because peoples' knowledge is not static, rather it is the result of constant development and innovation reached it in the dwindling situation. Manchester politics of British on cotton production during nineteenth and twentieth century had killed the wisdom of family based weaving tradition. Ignorance of National Government detected homegrown weaving technology as subjects of arts, aesthetics, identity symbols, and cottage industry. The potentialities of women in hill areas who had primary technological knowledge on a production system and who were self-dependent in their weaving production technology could not be considered as very potential human resource for further prosperity and development of nation. Somehow, different programmes of small-scale industries, small-scale loan, welfare schemes, regenerated wisdom of rural women in transition. However, no steady links are established between big textile industries and the women who had knowledge of weaving of cotton, silk, fibre, *endi* garment materials, all types of cloths, necessary for furnishing, woolen cloths and carpets.

Small-scale Loans: A Few Case Studies

In the year 1993, February-March, when I enquired about welfare schemes on weaving in the Block Development Office of Demoria (Sonapur), District Kamrup, Assam, I came to know that women at village level are supplied yarns at subsidised rates. It was quite happy news and further inquiries revealed the fact that this facility is given to six women in a block, yearly. I hardly met any women who received this facility. Such situation needs no further comments. In one neighbouring village of Demoria Block Office, I came across a few women who had received yarns from a Marwari Welfare Organisation, free of cost. They use these yarns for commercial production and half of the production is given to the previously mentioned welfare society in lieu of yarns. This society is a regular purchaser of weaving products of commercial value in the village. Whether it can be taken as an ideal policy to promote the income skill of women or as beneficial in the long run?

Kamal (2000) published an evaluation on the minor loans/ small loans, an experience of Bangladesh. This is an outcome of a discussion on exchange of ideas, where they evaluated the existing problems and prospect of small-scale loans. This discussion is pivoted on three notions:

(a) The small loan givers are the moneylenders of new generation

(b) These moneylenders are strengthening the power of world capitalism.

(c) They are local representative of capitalists.

Government of India has many such programmes like goatery, piggery, poultry, and giving loan to purchase rickshaws. I have hardly met any such beneficiaries in the field surveys in West Garo Hills villages of Meghalaya; villages in Dimoria Block, Kokrajhar, Nalbari, Darrang in Assam and villages in Tirap district, Arunachal Pradesh, who could achieve some prosperity from such programmes.

In Assam and in Arunachal Pradesh cooperatives of women weavers are many in number. However, success stories of such cooperatives are extremely meager. In Arunachal Pradesh, Training Centers for Technical Education is imparting training of weaving to women in rural areas in fly shuttle looms. Nevertheless, in reality, I observed that the waist looms/ loin looms are much popular among the women than fly shuttle looms. In fact, waist looms are products of indigenous technology. Each aspect of it is a known area of knowledge for them. Fly shuttle looms are more productive, but not handy. Fly shuttle looms involve costs and are available in the market. In contrast, women use loin looms know the technology to make it and the raw materials of loin looms are available at home. Culturally loin looms are considered as women's property. Daughters carry their loin looms with them when they go to husband's house after marriage. Such an integrated system based on innovative indigenous knowledge not yet attracted our technologists, who could invent a mechanised variety of the same model of loin loom for the growth in production.

Ajad (1999) observes that small-scale loans can achieve success at a low level. Beneficiaries of small-scale loans cannot survive in the more competitive market, because many a time they cannot sell their products in the proper cost locally. They cannot send their production at markets of distant places. Many a time, it is found that the receivers of small-scale loans are lending the money to poorer people rather investing it in any business and earn interests. As a result, an unproductive section of moneylenders emerges in the society.

Still we have to keep ideas of Kamal (*ibid*) and Ajad (*ibid*) at level of scrutiny. However, their experiences may be applied to judge situations here. Women are enthusiastic to establish cooperatives for women weavers, where they have to produce lists of members, to get it registered and get loans. For purchasing of yarns they have to face a costly market and they say that they do not get buyers at remote villages. More success could have created a situation, which attracts women to this indigenous knowledge system day by day.

Aesthetics and Commerce

Immense potential in these productions attracted attentions of fashions designers and business persons in recent years, who are more interested to sell aesthetics in it. They are using sentiments of buyers who are crazy for ethnic designs and handloom products. These designers many a times use tribal motifs according to their own imagination or add some new ideas in it which is nothing but a mixture or an improvising of ethnic designs, originally created by tribal women in different communities in North East India. Big textile firms and industries are potential buyers of such designs. These industries sanction projects to work on ethnic designs. Such activities easily will eliminate weavers from weaving technology, because the small cooperatives in any case would not be potential competitors of big textile companies, who sell their products at international markets

Struggle to Defend Rights to Self-determination and Indigenous Women

I had visited government craft centre of Longding, Tirap district of Arunachal Pradesh on several occasions. This is a centre where trainees are trained in wood-carving and weaving. Trainer wood carvers are Wancho and it is traditional craft for them. The trainer in weaving is a man who received his Diploma from Bombay, and trained in fly shuttle loom. The women trainee attends classes are more or less exposed in weaving through loin looms before coming here. After completion of such training, very few of them purchase fly shuttle looms. The craft centre hardly has any other programme to maintain networks with these trainees. Besides, craft centre has a selling counter, where they sell products made by their trainees and the purchasers are people of locality, government employees and people like me who are very few in number. This centre could reach to larger market beyond their areas through district level and State level craft centre. The State's craft centre sells products of the different tribes from their only selling counter situated at the State capital at Itanagar. These crafts reach larger market only through a few National fairs, organised once or twice in a year. Just before attending any such National fairs, State's craft centre collects the best crafts from district level craft centers. From this example, one can understand well about the vast market where products of Arunachal Pradesh not yet reached within Nation. Such limited movement of industrial products can predict the longevity well. If not late, it calls for appropriate policies for weaving and weavers to ensure rights to the people to practice indigenous knowledge.

Post independent movements organised by several communities for political autonomy identified weaving products as symbols of heritage. The colourful woven products attracted many words of appreciation. All the communities in this region welcome their guests of honour. But does this heritage really haunt the mind of leaders of North East India to establish an institute related to weaving and textiles. Not a single faculty is introduced in any University of North East India for advance growth of such knowledge system which has deep root in Assam, Manipur, Nagaland, Mizoram, Arunachal Pradesh, Tripura and Meghalaya. None the social movements from district councils, autonomous councils to statehood considered it a potential resource in their region and put it in their agenda for development or at least in lists of demands. In post movement situation woven garments, being status symbol and identity symbol of Ministers and Government officials perhaps traveled far off places of the globe not as industrial products as woven by indigenous women.

Beijing Declaration of Indigenous Women

In the Fourth World Conference of Women, indigenous women drafted a proposal of demand where they demanded recognition and respect for their rights to their intellectual and cultural heritage and their rights to control the biological diversity in their territories. They appealed to TRIPS and GATT not to apply their own definitions to define indigenous peoples, communities and territories. World Trade Organisations must recognise their intellectual and cultural rights and asked safeguards from the domain of private intellectual rights and corporate monopolies. Through their demand when they wanted to protect right and respect for self determination , right to territories, bio-diversity to revitalise and rejuvenate their biological and cultural heritage and wanted to resume the positions of guardians and custodians of their knowledge and bio-diversity. It is not clear from this draft whether they have set forth an endangered perspective to establish their own right over production or not (from *Beijing Declaration of Indigenous Women*, 1995, 30 August – 8 September). If one, considers this proposal as more responsible step to establish rights to self-determination of indigenous people and compare it with the situation of third world, where women are fighting hand in hand with their male counterparts to establish their rights for political self-determination. Were they able to establish any right of indigenous women to practice their indigenous knowledge and technologies, for a better future? Were they able to establish the rights of women to their production. Alternatively, it has remained an unsolved agenda of women.

Indigenous women are fighting for respect and recognition of indigenous knowledge in International Women Forums for their own people. And at home Indigenous Women Organisations in North East India and researchers and activists are trying to solve the problems of women in the inheritance of property of father and husband (Dai, 2000 ; Marak, 2000 ; Barooah, 2000; Haloi, 2000 ; Singh, 2000; Marak, 2000; Sharma Thakur, 2000; Devi, 2000; Khiangte, 2000; Mipun, 2000).

Now the question which comes in mind is whether the indigenous women, will be able to decide their priority between heritage and right over production and knowledge what they have created from time immemorial. Indeed this is a crucial moment for them when they have to establish their entitlement on the questions of empowerment (right over indigenous knowledge) and custodian of territories.

Summing up

Indigenous knowledge or knowledge of the people of third world has not yet received the status of right to work for the development. Modern India as welfare state has introduced many programmes to assure a better life to the people assuming that the scientific knowledge of the post renaissance Europe would be only weapon to address development. As a result the women's knowledge was not taken as one of the resource of human development? Concepts of indigenous knowledge system, sustainable development may have changed the direction to rethink some aspects related to development. But have such currents within the globalisation process been able to establish a knowledge system. We must agree to one aspect that the weaving technology, which is innovated and preserved for centuries by women and still surviving is not a heritage rather representative of an effective technology and as the knowledge of the collectivity.

References

Ajad, L., 1999, "Discourse of Economists and Sociologists", in M. Kamal (Ed) : *Small Scale Loans : Experience of Bangladesh,* pp. 14, Dhaka : Samaj Chetana Publishers.

Barooah, J., 2002, "Property Rights with Special Reference to Women in Tribal Areas". Proceedings of the Seminar on Property Rights with Special Reference to Inheritance Right Related to Women in Tribal Areas of North East India, held on 28-29 June, 2002 at NIPCCD, North East Regional Centre, Guwahati, Assam.

Beijing Declaration of Indigenous Women, 1995, NGO Forum United Nation's Fourth World Conference on Women, 30 August – 8 September 1995, Beijing.

Chaudhuri, S.S., 2002, "Social Context of Wancho Designs: Towards an Alternative Paradigm". *Journal of Indian Anthropological Society,* 51, 2: 103-120.

Dai, M., 2002, *Arunachal Pradesh : The Hidden Land,* New Delhi : Sky Printers Pvt. Ltd.

Devi, J., 2002, "Property Rights and the Status of Women among the Rengma Tribe of Nagaland: A Case Study of Tesminyu Village". Proceedings of the Seminar on Property Rights with Special Reference to Inheritance Right Related to Women in Tribal Areas of North East India, held in 28-29 June, 2002 at NIPCCD, North East Regional Centre, Guwahati, Assam.

Elwin, V., 1988, The Art of the North East Frontier, Itanagar: Directorate of Research, Government of Arunachal Pradesh.

Elwin, V., 1988a, A Philosophy for N.E.F.A., pp 35-66, Itanagar: Directorate of Research, Government of Arunachal Pradesh.

Ghosh, G.K. and S. Ghosh, 1997, Women of Manipur New Delhi: A.P.H. Publishing House.

Haloi, K., 2002, "Property Rights and Status of Women: A Case Study of an Angami Village of Nagaland". Proceedings of the Seminar on Property Rights with Special Reference to Inheritance Right Related to Women in Tribal Areas of North East India, held in 28-29 June, 2002 at NIPCCD, North East Regional Centre, Guwahati, Assam.

Kamal, M., 2000, *Small Scale Loans: Experience of Bangladesh*. Dhaka: Samaj Chetana Publishers.

Khiangte, L., 2002, "Property Rights with Special Reference to Inheritance Rights of Women in Mizo Society". Proceedings of the Seminar on Property Rights with Special Reference to Inheritance Right Related to Women in Tribal Areas of North East India, held in 28-29 June, 2002 at NIPCCD, North East Regional Centre, Guwahati, Assam.

Marak, L.R., 2002, "Property Rights of Women and Inheritance in Garo Society". Proceedings of the Seminar on Property Rights with Special Reference to Inheritance Right Related to Women in Tribal Areas of North East India, held in 28-29 June, 2002 at NIPCCD, North East Regional Centre, Guwahati, Assam.

Mipun, J., 2002, "Property Rights with Special Reference to Inheritance Rights of Women among the Mishing Tribe of Assam". Proceedings of the Seminar on Property Rights with Special Reference to Inheritance Right Related to Women in Tribal Areas of North East India, held in 28-29 June, 2002 at NIPCCD, North East Regional Centre, Guwahati, Assam.

Roy, N., 1979, *Art of Manipur.* Delhi : Agom Kala Prakashan.

Sharma Thakur, G. C., 2002, "Property Rights with Special Reference to Inheritance Rights of Women in the Boro Kachari Society of Assam". Proceedings of the Seminar on Property Rights with Special Reference to Inheritance Right Related to Women in Tribal Areas of North East India, held in 28-29 June, 2002 at NIPCCD, North East Regional Centre, Guwahati, Assam.

Singh, C. N., 2002, "Inheritance Rights of the Tribal Women of Manipur". Proceedings of the Seminar on Property Rights with Special Reference to Inheritance Right Related to Women in Tribal Areas of North East India, held in 28-29 June, 2002 at NIPCCD, North East Regional Centre, Guwahati, Assam.

Singh, R. K. R., 2002, "Pattern of Inheritance among the Tribes of Manipur". Proceedings of the Seminar on Property Rights with Special Reference to Inheritance Right Related tc Women in Tribal Areas of North East India, held in 28-29 June, 2002 at NIPCCD, North East Regional Centre, Guwahati, Assam.

4

The Indigenous Knowledge System of the Lotha Nagas with Specific Reference to the Knowledge of Matching Paddy Types to Varying Soil Types

K.M. Francis

This account is a study of the indigenous knowledge system of the Lotha Nagas with particular reference to the knowledge of matching paddy types to varying soil types and climates. This particular facet of the knowledge system of the Lotha Nagas is focused because of the centrality of this knowledge base for the very survival of the people, as 90 percent of the people depend on paddy cultivation to meet their subsistence needs.

Besides discussion on the soil, types and the varieties of paddy grown in the Lotha Naga area, the study is contextualised with reference to the relevant customs and practices associated with the particular pattern of cultivation called *Jhumming* engaged in by the people at large. The sufficiency as well as the efficiency of the knowledge base is also ascertained by estimating the yield taking into account the investment of energy and capital in terms of human labour and expenditure for feast giving and ceremonies associated with food production.

The data covering the subject matter is collected by staying in the selected sample villages during different working seasons, observing the seasonal activities and often participating in

Jhumming and other economic and social-cultural activities along with the villagers. Besides the participant-observation method, a number of farmers were interviewed.

The Lotha Naga tribe is one of the major Naga tribes, which occupies the mid-western part of Nagaland. The Lotha Naga tribe with it's headquarter at Wokha covers an area of 1,628.00 sq. km. bounded by Assam on the West, Mokokchung district on the North, Zunheboto district on East and Tseminyu subdivision in the South. The district is made up of three ranges, namely: Upper, Middle and Lower.

The Lotha Nagas live in close intimacy with nature depending on it for their subsistence. They have an acute awareness and knowledge of the environment in which they live. There is a great store of traditional knowledge passed on from generation to generation. Every generation adds to that storehouse with their experience gathered through observation over many years of practice. Types of terrains, climatic conditions, soil types, suitability of various paddy varieties to various soil types are part of their store of knowledge. Even though great efforts are made to introduce cash crops and varieties of fruits, the rice and vegetables grown through *Jhumming* remains largely their resource base. The degree of control or modification of the natural environment is low as the people in the villages still rely on simple technology. Therefore, in the present context, they meet their sustenance needs by matching the paddy types with the various types of soil and climate.

Classification of Soil

The cultivator, after years of practice, knows well what type of soil is good for what variety of paddy. The people in general make three broad classifications of soil: *Likotso* (clayish soil), *Hachangli* (sandy soil) and *Longkroli* (stony soil). Presence or absence of sand in the soil gives rise to further classifications. The knowledge of the type of soil is important for the farmer, as he has to match the paddy type with the soil type for getting the best yield.

Likotso : This is a purely clayish soil. There is no sand in it. People check the presence or absence of sand with the teeth. The colour of *Likotso* could be black or red. This soil is very good for paddy. Generally, good varieties of paddy are sown in this soil. Even if there is no rain, it will keep the paddy alive. The paddy cultivated in this soil has a very good taste. Unlike other types of soil, in this type, paddy is cultivated consecutively twice. In the first year *Motso* varieties (late varieties) are planted, whereas in the second year *Moro varieties* (early varieties) are planted. This type of soil is most suitable for chilly and vegetables. Naga *Dal* and Maize also grow well in this soil.

Linyik : *Linyik* is a type of *likotso* but has some quantities of sand. This soil is considered the most fertile soil. This is a clayish soil, which is black in colour. This is the most suitable soil for paddy cultivation. Every kind of paddy grows well in this soil type. The growth rate of paddy is different in different regions because of the variations of climate and soil. With regard to sowing, the *Motso* varieties are sowed on time in March-April, whereas the *Moro* varieties are sown later in this type of soil, as the climate warms up. If the *Moro* varieties are sown at the same time as *Motso*, they will grow faster and the yield will be less. Therefore, the selection of the type of paddy has to synchronise with the climatic conditions and the type of soil.

Hachangaesemo : This is a sandy soil and not fertile. It is found that in the initial stages, the crop grows well, but as time goes, it is stunted. Being sandy, the soil is easily washed away during the rainy season and hence does not retain the fertility. This soil is seldom cultivated. Only those who do not have sufficient good soil will cultivate this soil. This type of soil is more frequently found in the lower range. Since the fallow season in this range is longer, the yield is quite good. Mostly only *Moro* varieties are planted in this soil. According to some farmers, among the *Motso* varieties, only *Maloken* and *Motiro* are found to grow in this soil.

Hachang Ochuo or *Harchang Lipomo :* This soil is blackish and moist. It is generally a low-lying area. In this soil, there is presence of decayed leaves. Here the sand will be of smaller size. This soil is used for planting paddy as well as vegetables. This soil is suitable for all types of *Motso*.

Longrokhyuli : This is a soil having large collection of stone. In between the collection of stones, the soil is very good. This is the type of soil best suitable for vegetables. Yams, beans, pumpkins, brinjal, chilly, ladyfinger, cucumber, papaya, bananas are planted in this type of soil.

Types of Paddy

Two general categories of paddy are *Moro* and *Motso*. *Motso* is a late variety, which takes about an average of seven months whereas *Moro* takes about an average of six months to mature. In the lower range, some *Moro* varieties are harvested in 4-5 months. *Moro* is smaller, whereas the *Motso* is bigger in size. *Motso* is planted in the most fertile places whereas *Moro* is planted in less fertile areas. *Motso* tastes better and hence people tend to have larger appetite for *Motso*. Because of this even if there is good harvest, rice gets over faster. Therefore, people with large families prefer to grow *Moro,* as they tend to last longer. According to people, three cups of *Moro* when cooked can be hardly finished by three people, whereas three cups of *Motso* when cooked will not be sufficient for three people. Big and poor families generally grow the *Moro* variety, whereas the middle and upper middle class families cultivate the *Motso* varieties. Below only the most common varieties of paddy are discussed. In keeping with the nature of *Jhum* cultivation, all these varieties are meant for dry cultivation on the hills, dependent purely on the rain.

Most of the varieties of paddy are sown in the month of March in the upper range and in the month of April in lower range. As the climate of the lower range is warmer, the paddy takes shorter time to yield than the middle and the upper ranges.

Varieties of *Moro*

Mangen / Nsa / Mesa / Era Mesa : This is the most popular paddy grown in practically all the villages. Most of the Lotha Naga inhabited areas are suitable for the cultivation of this paddy. The colour of the husk is light brown, while the rice is red in colour. It is small, hard and sweet. When other varieties of paddy are not suitable, this variety is grown. Since this variety can grow anywhere, it is also called *Nsa*. This variety is generally sown in the month of March. It grows to an average height of 120-125 centimeters. The average number of tillers per seed is 4-5 tillers. Generally, this variety has the highest number of tillers. It takes an average of 175-180 days to be ready for harvesting. The seeds sown per hectare are an average of 42 kilograms and the yield per hectare is 14-15 quintals.

Kuki Moro: The cover is red, but the rice is white in colour. It is small and grows everywhere. The best time to sow is in the month of March. It grows to an average height of 120-135 centimeters. The average number of tillers per seed is 4-5 tillers. It takes 175-180 days to be ready for harvesting. The seeds sown per hectare are an average of 48 kilograms, and the yield per hectare is 15-16 quintals.

Moro Tsok/Chothum : Some villages call this variety *Changki* as they have brought this variety from Changki village that is contiguous with the middle range of Lotha Naga area (Wokha district) in the Ao Naga territory in Mokokchung District. This paddy is the first to be harvested and hence it is called *Moro Tsok*. Around the field hut, *Moro Tsok* is planted so that it can be harvested first and the place can be cleared for threshing and winnowing. The best soil for planting, *Moro Tsok* is *hachangaesemo*. In other soil types, this variety will mature fast and the yield will be less.

Moro Epyo : This paddy has whitish cover and the rice is also white in colour. A special quality of this rice is that it is sticky when cooked as well as oily and hence this rice is popularly known as gum rice. It is also sweet. This paddy grows in all soil. This rice costs around Rs. 20 per kg. that is double of the other varieties. The three varieties of *Epyo* grown by the farmers, *Moro Epyo* and *Jaha Epyo,* are indigenous varieties, whereas *Mekheri Epyo* is considered to have been brought from Mikir Hills. *Jaha Epyo* has brown husk, whereas the rice is slightly black in colour.

Malen: This variety is of two types. *Malen Enhyumo* or *Moro Enhyumo* has red husk and white rice. *Malen Enhyumo* or *Moro Enhyumo* also has red husk as well as red rice. The *Malen* varieties are generally sown in March. It grows to an average of 120-125 cm height. The average number of tillers per seed is 4-6. It takes 175-185 days to be ready for harvesting. The seeds sown per hectare are an average of 48 kilograms and the yield per hectare is 14-15 quintals.

Nromo/Hoka : This is the smallest among the paddy. The husk as well as the rice is reddish. It grows well even in sandy and rocky land and hence generally planted in the poorest soil. The rice is quite hard when it is cooked and cooled. It takes about 120-130 days for harvesting. The seeds sown per hectare are an average of 48 kilograms and the yield per hectare is 14-15 quintals.

Varieties of *Motso*

Yanthungu : This is the king of paddy. It is soft and has good scent. This variety of rice is the most preferred variety of rice. The husk is red whereas the rice is white in colour. It grows only in the good soil. The best time for sowing this variety is the month of March. The average height of the paddy is 120-135 centimeters. The average number of tillers is 4-5 nos. per seed. The average duration is 195-205 days. The seeds sown per hectare are 48 kilograms. The average yield per hectare is 14-15 quintals. It grows well in *Linyik* type of soil.

Malenken/Maloken : This variety is also soft and has good scent. However, the scent goes away after sometime. The husk is brown and the rice is white in colour. There are also many villages, which grow this variety. This variety is preferred because the yield is good and the rice has good taste. Besides this variety can be stored for more than ten years as it is not susceptible to insect attacks. The best time for sowing this variety is the month of March. The average height of the paddy is 120-135 centimeters. The average number of tillers is 4-5 nos. per seed. The average duration 180 - 195 days. The seeds sown per hectare are 48 kilograms. The average yield per hectare is 14-15 quintals.

Shapvu : The husk is brown in colour, whereas the rice is white in colour. It is shorter than *Maloken*. It is soft and has no scent. This also can be stored for more than ten years as it is resistant to insect attacks. The best time for sowing this variety is the month of March. The average height of the paddy is 120-135 centimeters. The average duration is 200-135 centimeters. The average number of tillers is 4-5 nos. per seed. The average duration is 200-210 days, and hence, this is the last for harvesting. The seeds sown per hectare are 46-48 kilograms. The average yield per hectare is same as *Malenken*, that is, 14-15 quintals.

Motiro : It is round in shape and smallest in the family of *Motso*. The husk as well as the rice is white in colour. It is soft and has good taste. It is a high yielding variety among the *Motso*. One speciality of *Motiro* is that it grows well in all soil types. The best time for sowing is in the month of March. It grows to an average height of 120-125 centimeters. The number of tillers per seed is 4-5 tillers. It takes about 185-195 days to mature and harvest. The seed rate per hectare is 48 kilograms. The average yield per hectare is 16-17 quintals.

Rukhatang : The husk is red in colour and the rice is white in colour. The rice after cooking is soft. The paddy is short and fat. It also has good scent. It does not grow in either too hot or too cold zones, but in medium temperature. The best time for sowing is in the month of March. It grows to an average height of 125 centimeters. The number of tillers per seed is 6-7 tillers. It takes about 185-195 days to mature and harvest. The seed rate per hectare is 48 kilograms. The average yield per hectare is 16-17 quintals.

Some varieties of *Motso*, which are not so common, described below are

Khompemo : The husk is brown while the rice is white in colour. It is long and curved and has good smell. It grows well in quite warm place and hence it is sown in the driest land a person may have.

Kolor : The husk is brown and the rice is white in colour. It has a hairy projection and hence it gives a scratching sensation. Because of the allergic reaction on the body, this variety is not planted nowadays.

Lyngkhumvu : The husk as well as the rice is white in colour.

Amoru : The husk is red and has stripes. The rice is also red in colour.

Zakha **:** The husk is red in colour, but one end of it is black in colour. The rice is red in colour.

Thumpuk Tsuk **:** The husk is red in colour and has stripes. The rice is white in colour. It is tasty. The yield is quite low, and hence it is not so common.

Tssok Nyiko : The husk is black in colour and the rice is white in colour. It is soft and tastes good. The yield is quite low in the middle and upper range, and hence it is not so common in these ranges. However, in the lower range, since the fallow season is more, the soil is fertile and the yield is higher than the other ranges.

Khumtia : The husk is white whereas the rice is red in colour. It is tasty and yields well in upper range.

Chopvu/Chopvu Tsok : The husk is brown in colour and has wing like small projection on the cover. Because of the wing like projection, threshing is more difficult than other varieties of paddy. The rice is white in colour. It is sticky and has sweet taste. It also has a sweet smell. It grows better in warm climate.

Menyiko : The husk is partly white and partly black, whereas the rice is white. It is soft and tasty. It needs good soil to grow. The stalks are tender, the paddy falls off easily, and hence it is not cultivated so commonly.

Khateru : This is a long variety of paddy. The husk is whitish and stripped. The rice is white in colour.

Cross-breed Varieties

Balancing the human population and their subsistence resource has been a major preoccupation particularly in the recent decade. Their indigenous knowledge system helped them so far to cope up and balance the human population and their subsistence resource. With the rapid growth of population and the consequent change in the ratio between population and the available land and the soil showing signs of exhaustion due to the inability to keep it fallow to allow complete restoration of fertility, there is a gradual openness to modern science and technology.

The State Agriculture Research Station (SARS) at Yisemyong, Nagaland has been conducting experiments to raise varieties of paddy that are resistant to diseases and are good yielding. They have crossbred the local varieties, and three main crossbred varieties have been made available to the farmers of Wokha District. It has noticed that the yield is more than double compared to the local varieties, the genetic composition of which has not been tampered. They are as follows:

SARS 1 : It is sown in the month of May. It grows to an average height of 145-165 centimeters. It gives an average of 4-6 tillers per seed. The duration is 143 days. The seeds sown per hectare are 48 kilograms per hectare. The yield is 36 quintals per hectare.

SARS 2 : It is sown in the month of May. It grows to an average height of 145-150 centimeters. The tillers per seed are 5-7 tillers. It also takes 143 days for maturation. The seeds sown per hectare are 48 kilograms. The yield is 30 quintals per hectare.

SARS 7: It is sown in the month of April. The average height of the plant is 135 to 142 centimeters. It gives an average of 3-5 tillers per seed. It takes 152 days for maturation. The seeds sown per hectare are 50 kilograms and the yield per hectare is 24 quintals.

Efficiency of the Knowledge System

Just as in most simple societies, the economic activity of the Lotha Nagas is largely a social phenomenon. Besides the satisfaction of wants, understood in an economic sense, there are complexes of traditional factors such as beliefs, duties, obligations and social ambitions that motivate behaviour patterns connected with the production of food. The context of food production is therefore a context provided by a close interaction between the natural environment and the social environment. In the interaction between the natural environment and the social environment, the indigenous knowledge system works as a cement establishing linkages. The pattern of interaction is gradually recognised and established through trial and error, and over years of close observation and practice. To highlight this, the whole cycle of food production through the practice of *Jhumming* is analysed below.

The ceremonial jungle clearing for *Jhum* cultivation starts in the month of November and goes on until the month of January. The plot of land that is cleared for cultivation is the plot that has been left fallow for the longest period. The fallow season is 7-8 years in the lower range, 5-6 years in the middle range and 6 to 7 years in the upper range. In the sub-range of Englan, under the upper range, the fallow season is 5-6 years due to the increase in the pressure of the population on the land because of the acquisition of land by Doyang Hydro Electric Project. It can be said that the most fertile land of the sub-range of Englan have been now submerged by the project.

In the past the plots have been cultivated only once after the fallow period. Now due to the increasing pressure on the land, the fertile plots of the upper range are cultivated for two years consecutively, whereas the unfertile plots are cultivated only once. When the fallow season is less, the yield is less. Generally, in the middle range, the yield is becoming low, because the fallow season is less. Due to the plantations of trees and the increase of population, the cultivable land is becoming lesser and lesser.

The people ascertain the fertility of the soil by the health of the trees that grow on the plot during the fallow season as well as their previous experience of cultivating the soil.

It has been more or less ascertained that a family of seven members would need about 70-75 baskets (*Okhyak*) of paddy per year. The basket used for carrying paddy from the field is made of bamboo. It is a long cylindrical basket with a narrow bottom and a wide top, and carried on the head. It is known as *Okhyak*. Some villages measure paddy in terms of tins today. Roughly, two tins would be equivalent to one *Okhyak*.

The normal measurement of paddy for sowing is done with oil tins today. In the past it was done with a small basket named *Etuk*. Three *Etuk* would be two tins of paddy. Two measures of tin would be a medium *Okhyak*. A normal family would sow paddy measuring 5-6 tins. one tin of paddy would yield an average of 15-20 *Okhyak*, which is equivalent to 40 tins of paddy. About an average of an acre of land would be required to sow paddy measuring one tin. The land requirement and the yield vary from place to place.

Maximum paddy requirement per person per year is 12 *Okhyak* or 24 tins of paddy. One *Okhyak* of paddy would give about 16 kilograms of rice. Rice is measured with a small tin (*kakong*) while cooking. A *kakong* per person for each meal is the general calculation. A normal *kakong* would hold about 250 grams of rice.

Along with the exploration of the interaction between the natural environment and the social environment, the investment of labour and capital on a land that would be necessary to sow one measure of tin, and which would yield an average of 20 *Okhyak* (40 tins of paddy), is also calculated below to ascertain the efficiency of the particular knowledge system. For the purpose of our study, the area required to sow one tin of paddy is referred to as a plot.

At the time of jungle cutting and clearing, the trees are generally cut to the bottom with the exception of certain trees that grow straight. Those that grow straight are pruned and the top is cut, so that they could be used for creeper beans. Clearing the jungle of the area (a plot) that is required to sow one tin of paddy would require an average of 15 labour.

After cutting the jungle, the branches, leaves and grass are left for drying. The burning of the jungle will take place in the first week of March. Generally, the whole area is burned on the same day. The boundary of the area to be brought under cultivation is demarcated well and fire is set at the bottom and the top so that it does not spread to the forest. The leftovers after burning are cleared. Generally, 4-5 labour would be sufficient to do the clearing of the leftovers of a plot. In the hill areas, the effect of the sun and the wind causes the fast drying of the felled trees and plants and hence the number of people needed to clear the leftover will be less than those in the plain areas.

The day for sowing is fixed and sowing is done immediately after burning and clearing of the jungle. In the upper range, sowing is done in the month of March, whereas in the Lower range, sowing is done in the months of April-May. Sowing in a particular area in which 5 to 6 tins of paddy are sown is done on the same day, which would require 35-40 people. Therefore, labour requirement for sowing one tin of paddy would be an average of 8 people. The labour requirement for sowing will greatly depend upon the type of soil. *Likotso* will require approximately 9-10 people per plot since the soil is clayish. *Linyik* will require approximately 8-9 people, since the soil is softer than *Likotso*. *Hachangesemo* and *Hanchang Ochuo* or *Hachang Lipomo* would require and least number of people that is 5-6 people. *Longro Khyuli* would require around 14-15 people.

Generally, the clan members and neighbours are invited to join for sowing. Often sowing, weeding and harvesting is done as teamwork. The team (*yinga*) would be formed according to the *Khel* (division of a village). There are four major teams (*yinga*) called *Epoe yinga* or men group, *Eloe yinga* or women group, *Loroe yinga* or group of young girls and *Khyingroe yinga* or group of young boys. The *Loroe yinga* and *Khyingroe yinga* are often groups of the same age-mates. The help that is given would be reciprocated for every field.

Sowing is done in a uniform manner. The Lotha Nagas follow a particular pattern of sowing called the *Nchuechum* method, following the fireplace model. The stones in the hearth are placed in a triangle. Digging and sowing is also done in a triangular manner. Interestingly, this shows the close relation between food production and food preparation. The shower would hold a small hoe called *Choktsu* in the right hand and use it for making small holes to which 8-12 grains of paddy would be dropped with the left hand. A gap of about a foot is maintained on all sides from each hole. Since sowing is considered an important activity, all the showers would have to be feasted during the sowing. This would cost an average of Rs. 320 per plot.

More or less, after about a month, in April-May, there will be the first weeding and clearing of the growth of grass. The first weeding is called *Chumba*. The roots of the plants and grass that grow are pulled out and gathered in a place. For the first weeding, an average 7-8 person's work would be required per plot.

Before harvesting, weeding is done practically every month and hence a field is cleaned 4-5 times before the harvesting. The use of salt is slowly becoming widespread as a labour saving device as it prevents the growth of grass. With the use of salt, the weeding is now restricted to only about 2-3 times before harvesting. Some farmers who use salt in the land say that it has slightly affected the taste of the rice and some say that it makes the soil hard and unfertile. They have observed that the use of salt kills the earthworms and many other micro-organisms needed for the regeneration of the soil. Therefore, some landowners who lease out land to others for cultivation do not allow the use of salt.

The subsequent weeding is called *Rochon*. For each *Rochon,* an average of 20 persons' work would be required for every plot in which one tin of paddy is sown. The last *Rochon* is called *Lirhon*. This is the final weeding before the harvesting. In the *Lirhon*, the stalks will also have to be cleaned. Therefore, an average of 9-10 days labour would be required to weed prior to harvesting. Thus, for weeding alone would require an average of 75 days labour per plot required to sow one tin of paddy (7+20+20+20+8 = 75).

Prior to harvesting, there is a ceremony called *Ethan Etso* or eating of the new rice. A small portion is harvested to conduct this ceremony. In the past, *Ethan Etso* was an elaborate ceremony involving the village as a whole, the village priest fixed the date and ceremony was conducted as a village. Today the celebration is denomination-wise or restricted to each family. Since most families are Christians, the pastor is called to pray over the new rice before eating. This feast would cost a minimum of Rs. 300 per family.

Generally, most varieties of paddy are harvested in the months of August-October. In the lower range, harvesting is done in the month of August, whereas in the upper range, harvesting may go up to the month of October. Generally, the *Moro* (early variety) variety of paddy would be harvested in six months, whereas the *Motso* (late variety) variety will harvest after seven months. For harvesting and carrying, the paddy of a plot would require 5-6 people. Immediately after harvesting, threshing is done on the same day or the following day. For threshing, the paddy of a plot would require 5-6 people. Both harvesting and threshing are generally done in groups. People who come for harvesting and threshing will be treated specially with a good meal, tea and a lot of rice-beer. Since a plot would require 10-12 people for harvesting and threshing, a good meal with pork or chicken; tea and rice beer would cost a minimum of about Rs. 40 per person. Certain rich families will also kill a pig during the harvest season to feed the harvesters and threshers. Other meat is not generally given to those who come for harvesting and threshing. There is a belief that duck meat should not be eaten during the harvest, as it would bring bad harvest.

Transporting the paddy was done in stages, particularly if the area brought under cultivation is far away from the village. *Echen Ranki* or temporary store hut was made after every 2 km for the transport of paddy to the village. This temporary hut is made after each stage. From *Echen Ranki* to *Echen Ranki*, an average person can carry an average of six *Okhyak*. This would mean that if the paddy field is six km away from the village, the paddy produced from one plot would require an average of ten persons labour. Today, trucks and other vehicles are used to transport paddy, wherever the paddy fields are along the roadside. The roads that connect the district with other districts and places make the *Jhum* fields accessible to the people. The National Highway connects Wokha with Kohima and Mokokchung. In recent times, a new road from Wokha to Bokajan is under construction. Again, the road from Wokha to Merapani of Assam serves the people.

Today most villages have rice-mills and therefore husking is done in the mills. Husking a tin of paddy would cost Rs. 10 and hence husking 40 tins of paddy would cost around Rs. 400. However, if it were done manually, 10 persons labour would be required to husk 20 baskets (*Okhyak*) of rice. Generally husking is done only according to need. Before husking, the paddy is taken out of the granary, dried in the sun, and husked.

What is given in the Table 4.1 is just the average investment to produce 40 tins of paddy from a plot after sowing a tin of paddy. Since every tin gives 8 kilograms of rice, 40 tins of paddy would be 320 kilograms of rice. Therefore, the average

Table 4.1. Cost of Paddy Production

Activities Associated with Food production	*Needed Work-force*	*Wages*	*Food requirement*	*Total cost per plot*
Jungle clearing	15	(15x60) Rs. 900	Rs. 300	Rs. 1200
Burning and Cleaning before sowing	5	5xRs.60 Rs. 300	Rs. 100	Rs. 400
Sowing	8	8xRs.80 Rs. 640	Rs. 320 (Rs.40 per head)	Rs. 960
Weeding (5 times)	75	75xRs.60 Rs. 4500	Rs. 1500	Rs. 6000
Ethan Etso (Feast of eating the new rice)				Rs. 300
Harvesting and threshing	12	12xRs.90 Rs. 1080	Rs.600 (Rs.50 per head)	Rs. 1680
Transportation	10	10xRs.90 Rs. 900	Rs.500 (Rs.50 per head)	Rs. 1400
Husking				Rs. 400
Total cost to produce 40 tins of paddy from a plot				Rs. 12,340.00

cost per kilogram of rice would be Rs. 38.50. The study of the actual investment of energy and capital in terms of human labour and expenditure for feast giving and ceremonies shows the efficiency of the knowledge base to meet the problem of sustenance.

Conclusion

The Lotha Naga society is an agrarian society and 90% people depend on *Jhumming* for their survival. Their knowledge system in this area, which is a complex of the knowledge of the environment, which includes the soil and climate, of the mode of production, of the use of particular technology and the pattern of the investment of labour, of varieties of paddy, passed on from generation to generation satisfy the food requirements of the people, but does not adequately contribute to the accumulation of capital, and hence they remain on the subsistence level.

The context of food production is a context provided by a close interaction between the natural environment and the social environment. In the interaction between the natural environment and the social environment, the indigenous knowledge system works as cement. The knowledge system determines the pattern of interaction to a great extent. In the past, lavish feasts accompanied clearing of the jungle, sowing and harvesting. Today these feasts have become quite modest. Again in the past, clearing of the jungle, sowing, weeding and harvesting were collective activities, which involved a big number of people. Today many of these activities are done as a family, to reduce the expense of food production. As has been said earlier, balancing the human population and their subsistence resource is becoming a cause of great concern today.

The type of terrain, which is steep, and the non-availability of a constant supply of water, leaves the farmer with no alternative other than to resort to *Jhumming* depending on the ash and the rain. Again, due to increase in population and the consequent increase in the pressure on the land, the ratio is maintained today by reducing the fallow period. Since the fertility is gradually lost due to reduction in the fallow period, the level of food requirement can be maintained by an efficient knowledge system, which can better match the paddy variety with the soil and climate. Labour intensification and reduction in fallow period would only lead to diminishing returns and ultimate depletion of the resources needed to maintain the eco-system. The cross-bred varieties are recently introduced and hence it is too early to say how far they are pest resistant and sustainable in the given eco-system.

For centuries, the indigenous knowledge system has helped the people to deal with the problem of balancing the human population and their subsistence resource. With the change in the ratio between the population and the available land for cultivation, and the soil showing signs of deterioration, people are realizing the inadequacy of their knowledge system.

Therefore, science and technology must come in a big way to aid the farmers, to introduce not only high yielding sustainable varieties of paddy suited to the eco-system, but also introduce new technologies of production to take the farmers to higher levels of productivity and the consequent higher standard of living, without at the same time causing environmental degradation.

5

Ethno Medicinal Accounts of the Mao Nagas of Nagaland

Lorho Mary Maheo

Medicine is the term generally used to describe the art and science of the prevention and cure of diseases. Ethno medicine or folk medicine is one where the system of cure and causation of diseases is not derived from Western medicine or any other systems of the great tradition. It is the term used for micro-level medical system.

Any system of medicine and the incidence of illness are particular to a specific social system. The tribal societies have their own systems of treating diseases and ailments. Interestingly enough certain illness is believed to be caused by evil spirits or certain super natural powers.

The knowledge of diseases, their classification and etiology i.e., a part of all cultural systems and ways of curing the disease and the same rudimentary medical knowledge is part of the enculturation of an individual. This is practiced at home in the form of preliminary medical treatment or what is commonly called "home remedies". The domain of ethno medicine is indigenous medical features those to which Bakhru (1992) refers as beliefs and practices relating to disease, which are the products of indigenous cultural developments not explicitly, derived from the conceptual treatment of modern medicine.

Of the 33 Government recognised Scheduled Tribes of Manipur, the Mao Naga tribe is one of them and inhabits the northern part of the State. They are mainly concentrated in the Senapati district. The Angami, Rengma and the Chakhesang Naga tribe in the North; the Maram and Zemi Naga tribe in the West; the Poumai and Tangkhul Nagas in the East and the Meiteis in the South, bound the Mao tribe. Some researchers considered the Mao, Chakhesang and Angami as kindred tribes while others described them as quasi Angami tribes (Kabui, 1993). According to the 1991 Census, the population of the Mao tribe was 50,715.

The Maos are generally agriculturists. They cultivate varieties of vegetables. They inhabit the land, which has a rich, and varied vegetation as the area stretches along the foothills of Mt. Esii on the Japfii mountain range in the west. The people have a close ecological relationship for they almost depend entirely on the mother earth for their sustenance. They collect their food, fuel, fodder, housing materials and herbal medicines from the forests where they live.

Following are some of the Mao's ways of confronting the different ailments using the home remedies and other local medicine.

Fever: A type of herb locally called as *Shemaki Pro* is usually administered to the patient in a raw form i.e. by plucking some leaves and crushing it or it can be boiled in water. The water is then used for drinking from time to time. This preparation must have been given to patients having intermittent fever (now diagnosed as Malaria) since long, which is indicated by the name of the plant (*She* – intermittent, *maki* – fever, *pro* – medicine).

The leaves of *Chittho-Nghii* (Neem, *Azadirachta indica)* is also used to bring down the temperature. It is boiled in water to which a pinch of salt is added and given to drink. Even for infants 2/3 spoonful is given. The same preparation may also be used for sponging purposes. *Totsupa nghii* (*Adhatoda sp.)* also used. The leaves as well as the flowers are boiled and the water given to drink.

Head-ache : To cure head ache or to get temporary relief from it the Mao people consume hot or pungent foods prepared with a mixture of either dried bitter gourd leaves (*Momordica dioica)*, garlic (*Allium sativum)*, *Kopfopro* (spring onion), sweet basil (*Ocimum basilicum),* leaves/fruits of Rosetta (*Hibiscus sabdariffa), Shiikho Kakhrii* - which is sour and sweet in taste, etc. along with or without fermented Soya been (*Glycime max)* in which ginger, chillies etc. are added to it. In some cases, massaging with/without mustard oil or pulling of some hairs is resorted to.

Throat pain: Besides consuming food prepared in the above-mentioned manner, gargling is also done with a pinch of salt. *Adhatoda vesica* is also sometimes boiled and the water, which gives a greenish tinge, is drunk from time to time. *Orashiikhokha (Solanum xanthocarpum)* is boiled in plain water. This is usually consumed in the morning. The term *Orashiikhokha* has been interpreted as God's brinjal. Hence, this plant is used for curing different types of ailments.

Cold and Cough: Garlic (*Allium sativum)* mashed with a pinch of salt with or without a few drops of mustard oil is rubbed on the palm. The palm is then warmed up and massage around the neck and chest region. The leaves of *Kholo Lochu* is mashed and applied on the neck and chest region. *Orashiikhokha (Solanum xanthocarpum)* is boiled either with water or it can be cooked and given to the patient. Fresh leaves of *Adhatoda vasica* are also boiled and given to drink after cooling it.

Diarrhoea and vomiting: Fruits such as banana *(Musa paradisiaca)*, wild fig etc are given. The tiny fruits of *Omoshii (Rhododendron succedanea)* are boiled with water and given to drink. The flower of *Rhododendron arboretum* is also boiled and given. The leaves of *Polygonum molle, Obeio (Polygonum orientale)* is cooked with rice and given. Boiled water with a pinch of salt added is also given to the patient from time to time. Sometimes gruel too is given.

For infants, the leaves of peach (*Prunus carmosiana)* is crushed on the palm and applied it on the anterior fontanel and on the sole.

Dysentery: The tender guava leaves (*Psidium guajava)* is boiled in water. The water is then drained out and given to drink. Tender leaves can also be taken (chewed) raw. The fruit if available is also given.

- The greenish outer layer of giant tree bean (*Purkia roxburghii)* is also boiled with water and given to drink after cooling it.
- A plant locally known as *Tobowo* is cooked along with rice and given to the patient from time to time.
- Varieties of other herbs such as Oxalis (*Oxalis corniculata)*, Shiiprii Priso *(Artemisia nilagirica)*, Japan Pro (*Eupatorium cannabinum)*- a type of plant believed to have been brought by the Japanese soldier during the World War II and has been named after it, etc. is boiled and given to drink.

Stomach Problem: Stomach problem can be of various types. Depending on the nature and the type of problem, different remedies are administered.

- If a person is suffering from stomachache – i.e., burning sensation following consumption of hot chilies, then something cold is applied on the abdomen region to give temporary relief. Cold water or sugar is also given. In some cases, a red-hot charcoal is taken from the hearth, drops it into a glass of cold water, and made to drink. Fresh soil taken and applied on the abdomen region also brings relief to stomach problem.
- For gastric problem or other formation of gases, the juice from the banana stem *(Musa paradisiacal)* is squeezed out and given to drink. Also a root of a type of wild berry (*Somososhii*) – a thorny shrub which is very bitter in taste, is crushed and mixed with water and given to drink. Mint leaves (*Mentha spicata*), guava leaves (*Psidium guajava), Kholo Nghu*, etc are also given in raw form. Bitter gourd leaves (*Momordica dioica), Eupatorium cannabinum, Solanum xanthocarpum,* etc. is boiled with water and given to drink. The leaves of Passion fruit (*Passiflora edulis*), *Somososhii's* root are taken for any case of stomach problem.
- If a person has stomachache, which is colicky in nature, then the pain is suspected to be caused by evil eye. In such a case, the treatment is completely different. The left over food or any food item available from the

suspected person is secretly taken and given to the patient. The victim after consuming it gets ultimately relief of the colicky pain. In cases, where the left over food cannot be obtained or if the suspected cannot be easily identified then the root of raspberry (*Physalis minima*) is boiled with water and administered to the victim. In olden days from the suspected thatched roof house some pieces of straw is pulled out and burnt. The ashes so obtained is mixed with water and given to drink. This immediately brings relief as well as cure of his / her stomach pain. In addition, to prevent further weakening of the body a chicken of medium size is killed and consumed by the victim alone.

Wounds: For minor fresh wounds one of the most popular herbs used by the Mao people is that of the abundantly available plant *Eupatorium cannabium*. For this, the leaves are crushed and the sap so extracted is applied on the wound/injury. Such application hastens the clotting of blood and prevent from further bleeding. In many cases, saliva is also added to it while crushing for it is commonly believed among the Mao people that saliva has a quick healing touch. Plants like *Gynura angulosa, Gynura cusimbua, Changha Pa*, Indian pennywort (*Centella asiatica)*, etc. are also used in similar manner.

Constipation: Lukewarm limewater in which salt is added is generally given to drink. For children having constipation Lifebuoy soap is sliced into small pallets and pushed into the anal opening (orifice) of the child.

Sprain / Fracture: Castor leaves (*Ricimus communis)* is boiled and applied on the effected area. The fat of either leopard/ tiger/wild cat etc. or snake is heated and applied on the affected region with a light massage. In case of fracture – bamboo split is used for support. A type of bean locally known as *Hrala* cooked with salt, grind and given to the patient for speedy recovery especially in case of fracture.

Jaundice: The leaves of sensitive plant (*Mimosa pudica)* is boiled and given to drink. Sugarcane *(Saccharum officinarum)* juice is also given. In addition, the uncooked crab is crushed along with a little amount of water and the juice made out of that is given to the patient to drink.

Diabetes: The leaves of *Gynura angulosa* is boiled with water and given to drink frequently. Winged bean (*Psophocarpus tetragonolobus*) is also either taken in raw form or cooked. The local term for this bean *Chinnira Vu* is so named after the ailment.

Nose Bleeding: The leaves of *Shiprii Primii (Artemisia nilagarica)* is crushed and packed into nostril. Cold water is also applied on the forehead.

Burnt / Scald: Freshly sliced potato (*Solanum tubersum)* is placed on the affected part. The thinly sliced potato sucks in the blister and heels the wound quickly. A type of plant locally called *Makhi Khebu* is used. The stem of this plant is cut wherein a milky substance is exuded. The juice is applied on the burnt area. Green moss found in river water is collected and dried on the lid of the cooking pot. It is then placed on the wound to prevent infection.

The yolk of an egg is also applied on the affected region. Also fresh blood from chicken is applied directly on the affected part. The fur of flying squirrel (Beilo) is also placed on the affected area. Sometime ink used in fountain pen is also spread on the affected area. Salt mixed with saliva in the mouth is also sprayed on the burnt or scalded area.

Boil: Application of yeast on the mouth of the boil leads to quick pus formation. In addition, consumption of chicken meat is belief to hasten pus formation hence consumed by many.

Swelling of Joints due to Sprain / Dislocation: Hot water with salt is taken to be the best remedy for treating sprain/ dislocation. For this, a soft cloth dipped in the hot salty water and water wrung out is applied on the affected area for a number of times (Hot fomentation).

Foreign body (thorn prick): To remove thorn that is firmly embedded into the hands or legs, yeast is inserted into the entry wound to enable the pus to form whereby making the wound larger and easier to remove the thorn or any foreign particle. A type of creeper leaves locally called *Machiipfii Pfii* is also crushed and inserted into the entry wound. *Nopu Pro*, a strong smelling herb is also used.

Foreign body (Leech in the Nose) : A thorny shrub yellow-berried nightshade (*Solanum xanthoιarpum)* locally called *Sokha-a So*, the fruit of which is mashed and mixed with water and then poured inside the nostril thereby forcing the leech to come to the edge of the nostril.

Foreign Body (Fish bone struck in the throat): The flower of tree Rhododendron (*Rhododendron arboretum)* locally called KONGHOA PA either dried or fresh is taken in a raw form – chewed and then swallowed.

Blister / Lip sore: The leaves of *Kholo Nghu* is plucked and dusted in the hot ashes and then placed on the affected or diseased lip.

Carries / Tooth care: A small iron rod hafted to a bamboo handle is heated in the fire. The red-hot iron is then inserted into the cavity of the tooth with the belief that the heat generated by the iron rod will kill the germs. A tobacco leaf dusted in the hot ashes is also placed on the affected tooth/ teeth to relief pain. Oxalis (*Ozhe Pito*; *Oxalis corniculata)* – The leaves are mesh and placed on the area.

Halitosis (Foul breath): *Solanum xanthocarpum* – the tiny fruit of this is kept in the mouth and gradually chewed.

Cracked Feet: A tiny bulbous perennial herb (*Alliaecae* family) locally called *Okei* is used. The bulb of this plant is properly cleaned and mashed into a paste. The paste, which is slippery, is then packed into the cracked area at bedtime. The pork's fat is also used for applying in the crack region.

Urinary problem: Leaves of *Kholo Nghu* is taken either boiled or crushed leaves mixed with the water and drunk. Another herb locally called Dziipao (*Plantago crosa)* is boiled in water and drunk.

Wasp / Bee Sting: The stem of yam (*Allocasia sp.)* is cut and applied on the site of the sting to prevent Oedema. Fresh wet soil is also applied directly at the sting site.

Small Pox: Small pox, which is fully eradicated now, was prevalent in the society in early days. To combat this dreaded epidemic, the Mao people consumed a type of spring onion (*Allium sp.)* locally called *Kopfopro* which is named after the dreaded disease. *Allium cepa* is also boiled along with rice and consumed.

Chronic Debilitating Disease: Although the medical term cancer was not known in the earlier days, people suffering from very chronic debilitating ailments the bark of *Kaka Bu (Entada scandens)*, a kind of tree with long pods is boiled in the water. After boiling it, the water, when turned into reddish brown, is consumed from time to time after cooling it. This tree is not supposed to be planted and it is believed that the tree is found/grown in places wherein evil spirit dwell.

Another similar tree locally known as *Chadzh Shpro Khro* is also taken. The root, bark as well as the tender pod is used for such type of illness.

Eye infection / Mild Trauma: For eye infection, the first urine in the morning is collected and 1 to 2 drops is put into the eyes. In case of dirt/dust, entering into the eyes it is either washed with water and breast milk is squeezed out from the nursing mother and few drops is administered into the eyes. In case of mild trauma too, breast milk is administered and hot fomentation is carried out on the affected region.

Dog Bite: Whiskers from the same dog (i.e. the dog that bit the victim) is removed. It is burnt and the ashes applied on the bitten area. In addition, coin is used to place on the wound. *Shikri Biro (Colocassia sp.)* is also sometimes applied on the bitten area.

Snake Bite: Small earthworm (a variety of earthworm, which coils by itself) is cut alive and consumed. In addition, the fat removed from the same snake is applied on the wound.

Skin irritation caused by caterpillars: The caterpillar is crushed; the fluid so obtained is spread over the affected area.

Removal of Warts: In order to remove the ugly outgrowth i.e. warts from the hands and feet – a particular type of insect locally known as *Pfochokhe*, having a yellow body and a blue black wings is used. The insect's head is removed twisting it. The fluid exuded from it is applied on the already pricked wart.

De-worming: A peculiar type of small snail locally called *Osikho* is cooked and consumed in the evening for letting out the worm from the stomach the following morning.

Ringworm: Saliva collected in morning is applied on the region, which developed ringworm marks.

Blisters / Rashes in between the Toes: The stem of *Kedo pa (Datura suaveolens)* is cut and placed on the hot ashes. It is then placed immediately in between the affected toes. The soot (*Pikri Dzii*) usually found near the chimney is taken and mixed with water. It is then applied at the site.

Back Ache: Leaves of *Vuni Nito (Allium odurum)* dusted in hot ashes and placed on the area. Sometimes hot fomentation is also done in severe cases.

Tuberculosis: The Mao Nagas consider this disease (*Chathira Vu*) as an outcome of general body weakness. Hence, they used to look out for a better diet. Consumption of meat such as puppies and piglets are belief to increase the strength and energy of the person.

Sudden Death: The outcome of sudden death is usually attributed to the work of evil spirits. Hence, a *genna* is observed to appease the spirits.

After the invention of modern allopathic medicines if one comes to know that he / she has high blood pressure or any other diseases / ailments one generally takes precautionary measures. They revert to nature and seek the traditional herbal home remedies.

Keeping in view of the various types of home remedies and other local treatments available in the Mao community, it is obvious that due importance was given with regard to their ethno medicine. How effective the traditional treatment could be, it is best left to the people's discretion as it has been aptly stated by Murdock *et al.* (1998) 'that the medicine of other peoples however slight, un-systematised, or contaminated by scientifically untenable assumptions it may be in particular cases, invariably contains at least some elements of validated empirical knowledge".

A study conducted in 1995-96 in three Mao villages viz., Chowainu, Makhel and Punanamei reveals some interesting picture of the type of medical facility availed or resorted to by them. Of the 344 postnatal deaths recorded, 28.5% (98) were administered traditional treatment. About 24.1% (83) resorted to medical pluralism i.e. those who have resorted both to traditional as well as modern type of medical treatment, while 15.1% (52) availed the modern form of treatment. About 32.3% (111) did not receive any treatment owing to various reasons.

Further more, of the 1662 people (total population of the above-mentioned three villages) about 14.9% (397) were reported to be sick during the year 1995-96. Of these sick persons, mothers comprised of more than half i.e 58.7% (233) followed by the offspring 36.0% (193), while husbands comprised of only 5.3% (21). Of the mothers reported ill, the type of medical treatment resorted to vary. About 31.3% (73) mothers sought the modern treatment, 33.9% (79) resorted to medical pluralism while 18.9% (44) depended only on the ethno medicine. About 15.9% (37) reportedly did not get any treatment for their illness. From the findings, it can be concluded that the Mao people still have trust in their age-old ethno medicine.

The Mao people being settled amidst rich natural vegetation have numerous plants, which are of great medicinal value to them. The plants and herbs numbering in hundreds are used for treating different kinds of diseases and ailments. However, it is also to be noted that most of these herbs are kept in secret by them for once it becomes public the efficacy of the herb minimises. Therefore, a good number of herbs are yet to be made known.

In spite of the availability of modern medicine, till date, a good number of Mao people still adhere to the traditional method for curing their ailments which they believe do not have ill effects unlike the allopathic medicine which have given rise to side effects. Some of the informants shared that they are more dangerous than the disease they claim to cure. For people who are far away from hospitals and dispensaries, the traditional or local medicine seemed to be their only remedy. Apart from the herbal treatment, the Mao believe in the Supernatural Healing as well.

With the advent of Bio-medical system majority of the people have stopped approaching the local traditional practitioners in times of ailment. They instead preferred to consult with doctors whose cure is relatively fast and simpler.

In many cases when the local medicine or the traditional

treatment fails to cure them, they generally preferred to consult with people from the modern profession. However, the Mao still believes and continues to depend on the traditional medicine for curing the disease and ailments.

Plants are an integral part of nature. They are the life sustaining force on earth. Scientists in many parts of the world have carried out extensive research and have proven to humanity the effective use of herbal medicine. Today, *Ayurveda*, the traditional medical practice of India has been well accepted worldwide. As rightly pointed out by Kurian (1995) ".... A retrospection of the healing power of plants and a return to natural remedies is the need of our time".

References

Bakhru, H.K.,1992, *Herbs That Heal : Natural Remedies for Good Health.*Delhi : Orient Paper Back

Kabui, G., 1993, *Genesis of the Ethnoses of Nagas and Kuki-Chin.* Kohima: The Naga Students' Federation, Nagaland.

Kurian, J.C., 1995, *Plants That Heal,* Pune: Oriental Watchman Publishing House.

Murdock, G.P.; S.F.Wilson and F. Violetta, 1998, "World Distribution of Theories of Illness", in S.M.Channa (Ed) : *Medical Anthropology: Health Healers and Culture,* pp. 247-76, Delhi : Cosmo Publications.

6

The House Type of the Garos– Its Technological and Cultural Backgrounds

Sankar Kumar Roy

The indigenous architecture is called sometimes vernaculars architecture. It is an important segment of ethno-science that enables us to understand the 'life and culture' of the so called 'primitives or the simple societies'. It is an artificially created environment within the natural environment. It is something like textiles that form an out cover on the body. The basic difference between the two is a textile is exclusively for a person, whereas a house is for all family members. It is a universal cultural response to the basic needs for achieving safety and comforts, more or less in the same manner all over the world. Basic structures remain same, but their morphological variations, minor or major, are observed even between two closely stationed ethnic groups under same ecological conditions. The morphological variation could be due to the difference in cultural aesthetics. This is a means to maintain cultural individuality or distinctiveness. The architectural homogeneity of any group is the reflection of its homogeneity in cultural aesthetics, knowledge and systems. In an indigenous knowledge system material and non-material aspects are indiscreetly interlinked and structured. Material or structural aspect of house has its non-material counterparts. These two together make the complete whole. Against this framework, let us examine the traditional Garo-house.

Topography and House Type

Nagaland comes under sub-tropical zone. It consists of undulated hills, and is crisscrossed by innumerable streams and streamlets. The deciduous vegetation forms a carpet over the hill surface.

The settlement complex of the Garos ethnic group presents a homogeneity and uniformity in its formation; variations if there be any are very little. The texture of the complex is as such: (i) Residential unit consisting of living house (permanent) and (ii) granary and bachelors' dormitory and (iii) Field house temporarily built for watching over the crops from being damaged by the wild animals. The Garo settlements are generally built on the depression of hills (Playfair, 1909). This is unlike other ethnic groups of North East India, *viz* the Nagas (Hutton, 1921; Mills, 1921) who built fortified settlements on the highest points of the slopes of the hills. The front part of the living house remains three to four feet high above the ground while towards the back or rear part, the height of the piles increases as the surface slopes down. The length of the houses vary from one hundred feet to two hundred fifty feet and the breadth remains around forty feet (Playfair, 1909). The height varies from eleven to twelve feet.

The floor made of bamboo rests on the posts of *Sal* timber and their diameter varying from four to six inches, or sometimes more. The cross beam are set on the pillars and are tied with thick cane slips; over this there is a bamboo layer, this is being superimposed by bamboo matting. The beams are at different points and receive support from the posts notched or natural V-shaped branch; vertically and obliquely placed in order to transmit the weight of floor in a balanced manner. The platform on one-side remains extended for practical reasons.

The walls are made of same type of matting as is used on the floor. They are supported from outside by the bamboo of moderate thickness, vertically and horizontally. The bamboo that gives horizontal support passes through the holes of the bamboo giving vertical support to the wall. Besides this, strong bamboo strips are there to reinforce the strength of the matting of the walls.

The roof is angular and composed of two frames made by strong but slender bamboo arranged in squares, tied by bamboo slip and thatched with grass, bamboo and cane leaves; of there grass is preferred most. The grass or bamboo leaves get rotten early and these need replacement at an interval of two years. This is done within a day by drafting man-days together from the male members of one's own clan with an obligation to reciprocate in needs.

The whole structure may be divided into two: the front door is not made on platform (*nokrra*). It is on the surface. This part is meant for the placement of pounder and pestle for paddy. This part occupies comparatively a little space. In front of this, a wooden carved out anthropomorphic *(Kima)* ancestral figure is erected. Next two or three steps up on to platform this leads one to main room *(nokgaehi),* the public room of the family; it covers one third of the whole building. Partition is absent but the space is divided into well-defined area.

At the foot of center, the post nearest to the door is the abode of spirit and the rituals centering round the spirit are performed inside the door. This place is called *maljure*. Next post, the center of the house *(chusimara)* is specified for the preparation of liquor and for fresh brewing. Further, on, there is a hearth, covering an area of four square feet having a depth of three inches within a wooden frame. Earth is laid on the bed consisting of plantain leaves on bamboo floor in order to prevent it from catchy fire. There is no chimney, but the smoke escapes out through the eaves. Over the fireplace a berth of bamboo, matting (*ongal*) supported by four-bamboo posts is made for keeping cooking utensils.

Beyond the fireplace, an area is specified for taking meals. Here the unmarried girls sleep on the floor. Here, there is no partition. During the pollution period she need not be in isolation, she remains with others. The last room *(nokdring ordun)* is the sleeping apartment of the owner. Among the Garo the owner of the property including house is wife. Beyond their apartment, there is a small balcony or *varandah.* Daughter when get married exclusively for one (future heir of property), a space is portioned off for the married couple in the main room. Except door, there is no window in the traditional house.

At one side of the *nokdring* is a latrine. This is the set pattern for house. If any one wants to have additional window, door, or platform, one has to pay for such privilege to the villagers by organising feast.

House building starts with song and sacrifice to appease the spirit and addressing him to bind strong and to consolidate the work of the builder. To understand the house type of this ethnic group the bachelor dormitory *(nokpanthe)* and tree house (*borang*) are to be taken into consideration. The *Nokpanthe* is quite high above the ground and the height of the platform varies from four to five feet above the ground. The staircases are made on a thick log by notching. There hangs a long cane to support the climber. This is meant for the male youths to spend the night in dormitory. The heavy and robust structure of the *nokpanthe* is built by using strong wooden posts and cross beams. The main post of the structure is decorated with the carved and coloured reliefs of tiger, fruits and vegetables. The village meetings are organised in the dormitory. Apart from that, the strangers are accommodated here for stay in night. This is a center of socialisation and training and recreation for the unmarried youth and this is the shelter for male youth at night until he gets married.

The *borung* is temporarily built tree house to keep watch over the agricultural field from damage caused by the wild elephants. Strong branches numbering three to four above 20 to 30 feet from the ground are lopped. Where on a structure of ten to twelve feet is built. This is connected with the ground by a bamboo ladder.

Some Aspects of Architecture

The existing technology applied in the interior area reflects even today the repetition of the experiences and knowledge that this ethnic group they inherit from their fathers or ancestors. It appears simple, but proves most effective under the given ecological condition. Some examples of the ethnic technology is in the relation between the wooden post and cane slip and bamboo and bamboo slip. The main wooden posts are very often tied with main beams by using cane slip. This is done so that the flexible cane knots can carry heavy weight and withstand better tension. One of the most important property of the cane slips is that during humid conditions (i.e. rainy session) it absorbs optimum quantity of moisture and expands; during dry season, it acts reverse. Thus, it offers flexibility sequentially it does not get rotten easily as the knot remains relatively protected from the rain and sun under this shade of roofs.

The *Sal* posts or the posts from other wood face the same consequences as the cane slips do. So during summer or rainy and dry or cold seasons the cane knot and the post expands and contracts or shrinks in a more or less equal proportion, because the relative organic properties of the two does not vary much from each other.The knots do not get loosened and thus a uniform strength in grip is maintained.

In the same manner the frame of the roofs made of bamboo are tied with the knots made of bamboo slips. Because of the homogeneity in constituents, during summer or winter both the bamboo, sticks and the knots expand and contract in an equal proportion; thus, the grips of the knot and its strength do not change; it remains same throughout the seasons.

The oven is placed in the centér, over that the vegetables and other organic materials are kept. The fumes created while cooking and smokes created roll within the room; it finds vent only through the eaves of the mat walls. This acts as a repellent to the insets and saves the organic materials from being infected causing and causing damage to the organic objects. The bamboo mat and the straw roof prove bad conductors heat. This keeps the room temperature more or less constant throughout the season.

The rear part of the house relatively remains always high above the surface for two reasons: Firstly, the pigs keep readily clear off the night soils discharged. These animals act as a scavenger and are consumed in celebration. What is felt that a cycle is maintained.

Another feature of the residential house complex is that the granaries are constructed separately together in cluster away from the residential houses. They give an appearance of small huts. This is done in order to save it from the accidental firing of the houses. The structure of granary stands on such a base carved out in a shape of mushroom. Such a shape is given so that the rats do not find a grip for climbing. Nowaday, instead of carved out mushroom base, the big boulders are used whereon the structure is set or placed.

A village or house gets more amenable to fire. It may be accidental or as a consequence to '*Jhum* operation' during the winter when the humidity level in the atmosphere remains extremely low. In order to avert the danger of the spread of fire from *jhum* field into the village, the possible points of intension are located. Such spaces are cleared off the herbs and the grasses and a number of firebreaks are created. The females conduct this operation with their children who are tabooed to take part in tree felling as well as setting fire to the dried branches during the initial part of *jhum* operation. They stay behind the village to keep constant watch in order to avert such an accident.

The granaries of individual families are built in clusters away from residential houses with an expectation that a house may burn accidentally, but the paddy for the rest of the season will be saved. They may build a house instantly but paddy cannot be procured so quickly.

If we look at the extended space on the one side of the platform of residential house, at first glance, it appears to have no functional end; but during afternoon, its efficacy was understood. Observed that lady carrying a basket on her back full of paddy; the tension of the basket remains on her forehead with a cane plaited band, came closer to the extended platform; moved back towards the platform, slightly knelt down, released the weight of carrying basket on the platform and got herself fully relaxed. For this, she required no help Moreover, she also cannot get help, as all are mostly busy in their own works. The families are nuclear and small ones, where working force is low. It is observed the platform remains a little below or at the same level of her hip and it maintains an average height which proves optimum for all. Therefore, everything has a tacit balance that keeps conformity with other functional aspects of the house.

Conception of House

To an Achik or a Garo a house not merely stands as an arrangement of some inanimate objects in a systematic manner;

it is something more than that, when he develops sense, he feels and sees it as a safe place of protection that is next to his lap or back of his mother (Roy, 1992). In the house, he keeps specific area reserved at the entrance for the spirit who protects the members of a family from the evils (Playfair, 1909). He is as important as his other family members are.

His mindset towards, society and culture develops within this artificially created environment. He sees the structural relation among the materials; he discovers the function and relation between the knots and bamboo and their forms and types and the variable roles of each in the construction of the structure. Through the construction of a structure, a Garo youth enters into the domain of the system of ethno-science without his knowledge. Everything is imprinted in his memory. This is termed as 'mental template' (Thomas, 1974: 12). when needed, the data he preserved in his memory in the form of 'template' becomes active instantly. His sensory and mortar nerves under the command of 'template' give visual or concrete shape to imagination or ideas. That's why it is seen that a Garo, whether young or old sits with bamboo or cane and iron chopper to meet his required or assigned expertise, he could imagine what should be sise and diameter of the bamboo at what point it should be notched; where the socket to be made; what degree the supporting angle the beam will be efficient to transmit the weight of the load on it in the form of roofs and withstand the blow of wind against it. Everything he learns through trial and error methods. Experiences are accumulated in his memory over the ages. The same gets stored in the form of concept and concepts are transformed into symbol.

To illustrate this personal observation as an example is cited from Rengiri in the year 1970. This is as such: I had a chance to see the process of renovation of a living residence. The male members of the clan collected bamboo from the forest owned by their clan. Some were busy in preparing the angular beams for the roof. Some were taking off bamboo slips with their multipurpose iron chopper (*Ate*), weaving mat for the walls and the floor that need replacement. The old were taking bamboo slips, of required measurements and number for making knots for light frame and supports and others had been within his vision. One knew one's assigned work; one had clear and distinct imagination of one's role to be discharged. In fact, one had cultural imagination for almost every item. Each worked in rhythm and harmony with other. The women served beer time-to-time, she also knew well when to serve. All knew the 'signs and symbol'. In appropriate occasion it works. It appeared a person acted as component of the system of this process. Mind and matter conglomerated together, a person merely acted as a medium.

All become a part of the same system. In fact, a Garo youth or an old repeat the previously set system in more or less same way. He hardly deviates from the traditional architectural pattern and in unchanged niche.

Why do they do so? Is it because of their confinement within the same environment for generations together or something else? To find out the cause it needs to take many aspects of Garo-culture into account; so, we are to go beyond the confine of material cultural aspects of settlement pattern. We are to examine the ethos and cultural sentiments centering round the house. We are to understand the relation between the residence and the person in light of customs, kinship system, inheritance pattern, etc. This is eventually examined in relation to the social structure with special reference to marriage system and other socio-economic institutions (Roy, 1981, 1992). The traditional architecture, no doubt, is mechanical reflection of cultural system. A study into its forms and function takes it beyond its inanimate level. Its construction pattern or structure is guided by the dictate of a set of functional needs. It is a mechanical creation and aesthetic expression of this culture of the same time.

In Garo matrilineal system a *nok* (residence) must have a *nokrom* (husband) and his *nockne (*wife) and their lineage is reckoned in terms of mother's clan. A Garo village when newly built or groups in size; it is within the territorial limit of ones own homogeneous clan it extends the space for its own clan members. Its content, function, and structure remain to be a replica of the parent village. Why does it happen so? What is thought that residence or architecture being a material culture is a component of total cultural system but at the same time; it cradles the basic unit (i.e. family) of the cultural system in it.

Independent of other a component hardly undergoes modification. Garo social and economic institutions have remained unchanged in their traditional niche. In such state, a homogeneous mindset exists. This makes the vernacular architecture with its functional and cultural contents exist still today even after the wind of modernisation steadily hits traditional system.

If one wants to understand the house in relation to person, one must take the prevalent customs and the psychology of the youths and their involvement in their parental residence into account. After attaining maturity a youth has to spend the night, in *nokpante;* he becomes a stranger in his own house. He becomes a part of the dormitory unit along other youths of his clan. This has direct impact on the layout plan and the construction pattern of the residential house. Therefore, among the Garos, a house means an institution for the parents; where mother is owner of the movable and immovable property; home is one of them, one married future heir of residence and other unmarried daughters and children only. The question of guarding house of village when one attains old age does not arise; the youths in the dormitory take care of it in a manner as their father did while he was a bachelor. System repeats; so traditional architecture continues.

Conclusion

A baby when develops the sense of perception about the world around him; he develops the idea of his home first. Here within the semi-transparent state of his home his conception towards the world develops in a way as his parents did. He takes initially everything granted being a member of a family first, and then as a member of his culture. At dawn, he goes to the *'Jhum field'* and returns a little ahead of dusk.

This is a regular rhythm. He stands at a given point of stage what Mead (1972:31) termed as a 'post figurative stage', which a culture has to pass through. He repeats almost everything as has been done by his forbearers. A Garo thinks that there exists another hill that looks same as the hills where he lives. His day-to-day life within the traditional setting continues to repeat the same function; same social relation, same type of economic activities. The males dance the same

Wanggala (post harvest festival) in consonance with the same theme accompanied by same *mildong's* (the scum) strokes and tune of the flute played, the females dance in the same rhythmic steps as their mothers did. Nothing has changed in the system of kinship pattern, marriage pattern; a male comes to his wife's residence after his marriage to stay permanently with her; property passes on from mother to daughter; husband simply acts as a manager. The very dictate of matrilineal custom regulates his works and actions and his role in social-political economic organisation.

In fact, under given ecological conditions (physical and cultural) there is a system of a set of variables where one's mindset almost gets fixed. Any new imagination does not get new space for its expansion since the prehistoric mode of subsistence pattern in economy continues to remain same (Roy, 1981). Under the same unchanged system the architecture developed once during past continues to exist unchanged.

References

Hutton, J.H., 1921, *Angami Nagas*, London: MacMillan and Co. Ltd.

Mead, M., 1972, *Culture and Commitment:* London: Panther.

Mills, J.P., 1922, *The Lotha Nagas,* London: Macmillan and Co Ltd.

Playfair, M., 1909, *The Garos*, London: David Nutt and Co.

Roy, S.K., 1981, "Aspects of Neolithic Agriculture and Shifting Cultivation". *Asian Perspectives*. 24: 193-221.

Roy S.K., 1992, "Garo", in P. Hokins (Ed): *Encyclopedia of World Cultures,* pp. 81-84, Vol. III, Boston: C.K. Halls and Co.

Thomas, D.H., 1974, *Predicting the Past, New* York: Holt Rinehart Winston Inc.

7

Indigenous Knowledge System In Every Day Life– Some Observations on the Idu Mishmis of Arunachal Pradesh

Sarit Kumar Chaudhuri

Study of Indigenous Knowledge System has provided a veritable space for inter-disciplinary research. Indigenous Knowledge System does not necessarily mean knowledge of the indigenous people only but also to that of any other defined community. The term Indigenous Knowledge System delineates a cognitive structure in which theories and perceptions of nature and culture are conceptualised. The dynamics of Indigenous Knowledge System thus takes place in two different levels, namely, the cognitive level as well as empirical level (Brouwer, 2000). Indigenous knowledge also refers to as traditional or local wisdom, is emerging as a priority concern on the international environment and development agenda focusing on goals, such as, strengthening local community control over process of ecological, social and cultural change, revitalising traditional knowledge transmission within local communities and evaluating customary rules and practices that govern knowledge access. According to Agrawal (2002), 'Indigenous Knowledge has come to occupy a privilege position in discussions about how development can best be brought about so that finally, it really is in the interests of the poor and the marginalised'. Kalland (2000) opines, 'this interest in indigenous knowledge should be welcomed for several reasons.

First indigenous people possess extensive empirical knowledge about their environment. Secondly, they offer interpretations of empirical knowledge radically different from the conventional scientific paradigm. Finally, there are important lesions to be learnt by studying the working of indigenous resource management regimes'.

Present chapter is a humble attempt to underscore how far Indigenous Knowledge System as a concept becomes useful in understanding the day to day life of the traditional societies with reference to the Idu Mishmis, a small tribe of Arunachal Pradesh. It focuses on the nature of utilisation of resources by observing daily life of many Idu families under different villages.

Locating the Idu Mishmis

Idu Mishmi represents one of the small tribes of Arunachal Pradesh with population strength of 9,350 as per 2001 census. They are spread over the lower as well as upper Dibang valley districts of Arunachal Pradesh. In lower Dibang valley, they are in close contact with the Padams with whom they had trade relations. There is a great degree of altitudinal variation, which makes the climate of their habitation area moderate to cold. Their physical features reflect Mongoloid character and speak in Tibeto Burman language (Dutta Chaudhury, 1995; Baruah, 1960; Pulu, 1978). In most of the colonial literature and in *Ahom Burunji* they are referred as Chulikata Mishmi because of their cropped hair, which is still prevalent among the older generation village people. Along with this hairstyle, their textile, traditional house, big knife and the *Igus* (Shamans) constitute some of the identity markers of this tribe. Society is broadly divided into two sections *Aho* (master or a free man) and *Apho* (slave) which are further subdivided in number of exogamous clans, such as, Linggi, Mena, Pulu, Meto, Miso, Misu, Elapra, Tacho, Melo, Mendo, Meya, Mihu, Mithi, Umbre, Umpo, Umpre, Apora, Meme, Mepo, Mitaya, Menda, Michichi, Mele, Aprawe etc. Traditionally they practiced polygyny and depended to large extent on shifting hill cultivation though now many of them opted for wet cultivation depending on the availability of cultivable land. Hunting, gathering as well as fishing are also practiced by them. They were famous traders for which they went to Tibet as well as to the plains of Assam, especially Sadiya in search of salt, beads, weapons etc. They are closely linked with their surrounding ecosystem for their subsistence.

However, with the passage of time like other tribes of Arunachal Pradesh, Idus are also exposed to various forces of change, which is surfaced with the greater postcolonial administrative penetration in to these valleys, which lead them into the path of transition.

Traditional House

An Idu house is an excellent piece of traditional architecture length of which may vary from 40 to 150 feet made out of variety of bamboos and wooden posts available in surrounding forests. Questions of water source and defense remained as the prime concern for the selection of the site where a new house will be constructed.

Generally, the main post is made of two kinds of trees locally known as *Kane* and *Ngero*, which are durable and not easily decayed by being buried in earth. Floor walls and rafters are made of a large stemmed bamboo (*Abato*) available within the village itself. Beam is made from fir trees whereas sun grass is used for roofing purpose. For tying the posts and mats etc., they use cane (*Aruto*) as well as one kind of ropes made of tender bamboos called *Abato*. Strips are taken out from such bamboo with the help of the knife, which are dried over the fire for two or three months. However, before the actual day of construction such strips are taken out and soaked in water for three to four days.

The roof both in front and rear ends take parabolic shape and the whole construction need some skilled hands that are known as *Otala Andaiga* in Idu society. It may be note worthy to mention that for construction of such a traditional house their women members also take part very actively for digging holes, carrying thatching materials etc., besides cooking and distributing food stuffs and drinks to the participants for three four days. It may be mentioned that Idus strongly believe that bamboos need to be cut during the new moon phase otherwise there is a chance of evil attack which may turn the bamboos useless after sometime.

Internal structure of the house naturally reflects family relationship and the length of such house obviously reflect the number of wives an owner has. In response to the possibilities of blood feuds, which frequented old days, Idus used to place their front doors in such ways that while opening the front door it will create a vibration through the corridor, which alert the inmates. They take sufficient precautions to guard themselves from the danger and the exit door leading to the pig run serve as an escape route (Bhattacharjee, 1983).

Inside the house, the main room that is used for all the family members and even where guest or stranger can sit is quite big and hearth is located centrally. On the top of the hearth, we can find three layers of stacks each of which has specific purpose, such as, keeping firewood for drying, placing utensils of regular use, drying chilli, meat, spices etc. In fact, this is one of the most important places, where older and new generations meet each other, and exchange their knowledge orally.

Two types of mortar (*Elobe*) can be seen which are an excellent pieces of their artisanship. For pestle, generally they use a tree called *Ishumbo*, which is heavier and suitable for pounding job. In Anini area they used to keep such items inside their house because of extreme cold climate related to the high altitude whereas in lower altitudinal areas this is generally kept under the portico.

Granary

Generally two types of granaries can be found in Idu villages; one nearer to their household and another located within the cultivable field. These are generally rectangular and built on the bamboo made raised platform with wooden posts. At the junction of wooden post and bamboo, made floors round shaped wooden plates can be found which prevent rats to enter inside the granary. Granaries are the storehouse of not only the grains and seeds but also valuable movable properties, such as new clothes, beads and other ornaments etc., these are kept in different sizes of baskets made for specific purpose. Roofs are generally made of a specific variety of bamboo. Number of wives usually determines the number of granaries.

Utility Articles

A large number of articles, which can be traced in an Idu house, are precisely made of bamboo, cane, wood and gourd. These articles can be broadly classified into carrying, storing, and distributing food items. Two tables are given below which will reflect how Idus are using their surrounding resources to make various baskets and other utility goods which constitute material of their day-to-day life.

Idu make baskets for various purposes, such as, for using during the life cycle rituals and festivals etc. but one striking use of basket is for carrying child. Such similar basket is also used for carrying firewood and popularly known as *Awento*. This type of basket can be made by any member of the society either in the name of child to be born or after the birth of a baby. Such basket, which is especially made for carrying children, is not used for any other purposes. However, it may be used only when a child is two years old. During basketry works, they mostly follow twilled, hexagonal and coiled netting pattern. A table is given below in order to understand the local name of various baskets, their use and durability.

Table 7.1 : Indigenous Baskets

Local term	*Purpose*	*Material used*	*Durability*
ASHUNU	Used for carrying seeds	It is either made of cane (*Aruto*), bamboo (*Hichito*)	Lasts for 5-6 years
AGRAH	Used for carrying fire wood	It is made up of bamboos	2 - 3 years
KEAKHUTI	Grains are stored	Bamboo	2-3 years
KEARONGOA		It is less rigid twilled made of bamboo or cane	1-2 years
AKUTI	Basket with lid where meats and fish is kept	Made of bamboo and cane	5-6 years

contd...

Table 7.1 *contd...*

Local term	*Purpose*	*Material used*	*Durability*
ANDRONGA	Open basket where vegetables are kept	Bamboo	3-4 years
ECHINGA	Where raw millet is dried	Bamboo	2-3 years
APRO	Mat where grains are dried	Bamboo	2-3 years
ISINGRA	Small mat for drying purpose	Bamboo	1 year
AWENTO	Basket used to carry child	Bamboo strips	2-3 years
AJI	Basket used to squeeze out rice beer	Fine thread of bamboo	-
CHORONU	Used as winnowing *papad* (*Eka*)	Bamboo strips	2-3 years
EPENDO	*Dao* is covered with it	It can be made with either bamboo or cane	3-4 years
AYUKU	Fishing basket	Bamboo	2 -3 years
ETONDOPU	Chickens are kept	Bamboo	1- 2.5 years
AYAPRA	Fan	Bamboo rope	1- 2 years
ANDRONDRO	Small cylindrical basket which remain hung above fire place keep spoons, match box etc.	Bamboo	1-2 years
EPEYE	*Dola* (with its help grains cover are removed)	Bamboo	5-6 years
APOTOLUAK UTI	Hat specially worn by males	Bamboo and cane	5-6 years
ENTO	Bag worn at back side during hunting	Cane	6-7 years

The question of durability of such basketry items generally depends on mode of use. Out of these large numbers of above-mentioned basketry, some are made more durable for specific purpose and some less durable. For instance, a basket called *Amboapi* is made less durable for preserving or storing seeds, maize and is used for once only. Durability also adds to the cost of the basketry. Depending upon the durability, pattern followed, skill, and material used, basketry cost varied for example – *Agraah* made up of bamboos which is used for carrying fire wood cost less then that of *Asim* which is either made of cane or bamboo and last long. It costs up to Rupees three hundred to four hundred. *Amuju* is a basket specially used by priest cost more then Rupees one thousand. Depending on the types of basketry varities of bamboo such as *Angeyto*, *Mangeto*, *Abraton*, *Hichito* and *Elinto* are used by Idus. The varities of cane like *Aruto*, *Erato*, *Lakambota* and *Lakato* are used in preparation of basketries.

Obviously, there no special ways or methods of processing raw material like it is done in industries but they have certain ways of processing using their indigenous technique. Bamboo ropes are prepared at the time of basket making; it is never prepared earlier because tasks become very tough to carry out as bamboo are dried very easily and when dried it becomes brittle. However, cane ropes can be prepared before carrying out one's works. These ropes can be kept for long time by drying it in smoke. It is never brittle like bamboo ropes. Further, these dried ropes are kept few hours in water before it is used so that ropes are not so tight to handle while making basketries. These ropes are prepared simply with the help of *Dao*. In addition, the time taken for preparation of basket depends on the type of design followed and material availability.

Table 7.2 : Household Articles

English Name	*Local Name*	*Raw Material Used*	*Uses*
Mug	*Achipru*	Bamboo, handle made of cane	For all kind of drinks.
Tumbler	*Awongto*	Bamboo tube	- do -
Bamboo Tube	*Achambo*	Bamboo tube	For carrying water.

English Name	*Local Name*	*Raw Material Used*	*Uses*
Strainer	*Kaji*	Cane	For straining Rice beer.
Wooden Piece	*Hakochi*	Wooden	Chopping meat and preparing *chatni.*
Spoon	*Inupu*	Made from a variety of gourd. It is dried and the seeds are removed. It may last for 5 to 6 years, depending on the nature of use.	For pouring out water.
Tea Kettle	*Siapu*	Made of bamboo tube, which is used only once.	For boiling water or tea.
Spoon	*Adodphra*	Wooden and can last for 3 years	Used while preparing and serving food.
Spoon	*Ikkedi*	Wooden or bamboo	- do-
Tongs	*Atophra*	Bamboo, which lasts at least for 3 months.	For holding or gripping vessels while cooking.
Jug	*Akapu*	A variety of gourd.	For keeping wine and water.
Pot	*Phitipu*	A kind of rock that is gray in colour, found in northern hillside.	Used in earlier days for cooking.
Mortar	*Elombwe*	Hard Wood	For pounding grains on.
Pestle	*Ihunto*	Hard Wood	For pounding grains on.
Pig-feed	*Ilipe*	Wooden	For feeding pigs food.

English Name	*Local Name*	*Raw Material Used*	*Uses*
Knife	*Era-a*	It is made of Metal with wooden handle. Durability is 5 years	For cutting purpose.
Drilling instrument	*Nambow*	The rotable horizontal stick is made of bamboo, the vertical stick is made of wood, which is fixed and made to pass through a heavy cylindrical stone block. The bottom tip of the vertical stick is metallic.	To drill holes on wood as well as metals.
Plates	*Agroko*	It is made of bamboo. The local people make it.	Plates.
Salt container	*Pra Eproko*	Bamboo tube	For keeping salt.
Container	*Sinkala*	Made of a variety of gourd.	Used for keeping seeds or wine.
Digging stick	*Akowe or taboo*	Wood, bamboo and canes are used for handles. The metal portion is bought from the nearby markets.	For sowing seeds in *jhum* fields.
Axe	*Epa*	Metal portion is bought from Roing; while, the handles are made by the people themselves, from bamboo.	For cutting and chopping.
Broom	*Achapey*	The brush of the broom is made from twigs of bamboo. Handle is of bamboo or cane.	Sweeping and covering the seeds sown in *jhums*.

English Name	*Local Name*	*Raw Material Used*	*Uses*
Spade	*Jepoka*	Handle is made of bamboo or wood. Its metal portion is bought from Roing.	Agriculture
Kurpa	*Asopra*	- do -	Agriculture weeding
Dao	*Einche, Eunta, Ambrepra, Sisha*	- do -	Agriculture, ceremonial dress and war.
Plough	*Kalaneya*	Wooden. The pointed, bottom is metallic. It is bought from the market.	For tilling the soil.
Sickle	*Kassi*	The handle is made of wood or cane. Metal part is bought from the market.	Harvesting
Cross-bow	*Irika*	It has a wooden body. The trigger is made from ivory. It is prepared by the villagers themselves	Hunting
Spear	*Apa*	Made from *Alidi* tree found in the forest.	Hunting
Bow	*Elipra*	The string is made from cane and the bow is made of bamboo. The villagers themselves make it.	Hunting
Arrow	*Epipho*	The raw material for arrowhead is bought from the market. The wooden part is made of split bamboo. The arrowhead is called *Mralatha*, when smeared with poison. The remaining portion is called *Apoha*.	Hunting

English Name	*Local Name*	*Raw Material Used*	*Uses*
Quiver	*Ela-a*	Made of bamboo, with a cap weaved from cane.	For keeping arrows.
Fishing trap	*Ayuku*	It is made from bamboo found in the locality.	Fishing
Fishing net	*Sha*	It is made of nylon threads. It is bought from the market. It needs mending after some days, which they used to do by themselves.	Fishing
War coat	*Atondre*	Woven from nettle fibers.	War
Haversack	*Eto*	Made of cane and bamboo (weaved)	Bag for carrying things.
Rain shield for haversack	*Inju*	It is made from the fibers of a bark of tree called *Elombho.* These barks are soaked in water and are made into threads or fibers.	Long strips of fibers in thick layers cover its backside to protect the contents against rain.
Shield	*Alih*	It is made from cane, bamboo and wood, in the village itself.	-

Clothings

In every Idu house one will definitely find a small portable waist loom (*Ancheta*) which is placed at one side of the main room, mostly nearer to the windows from where sunlight may come during day time. Different structural components of this home made loom reveals that varieties of bamboo, cane, stem of betel nut tree, wood etc.; which are locally available are used for the construction. The knowledge of constructing such a simple loom as well as the art of weaving is handed down traditionally from mother to her daughters. Most of the Idu women in villages are expert weavers and their woven cloths remained one of the important items for trade, which were exchanged with the communities of hills and plains. Their typical motifs and colours became an identity marker for the Idu community as such. Traditionally they used to prepare clothes out of plants fiber. These are extracted from *Malu*, a nettle plant and *Nabe Embung*, a small shrub. These are collected from the forests and dried. The fibers are extracted and made into balls and then put into hot water. The ash of burnt wood is added to it and stirred with a ladle. The yarn is then taken out, washed, dried and put into the loom. They are also used to prepare three colour dyes, such as red, green and black from the plants available in the forests. During weaving, they use some whitish powder available on the surface of dry banana leaves (*Akona*) to keep the yarn smooth and it helps in faster movement of *Abipra*, a flat bamboo made structure used for weaving.

Another significant item of their traditional textile is their male war coat (*Atondre*) which can prevent the strike of a sword during war or feud. This is made of the bark fiber mixed with human hair. This is quite heavy (approximately 2 - 2.5 kg) and exclusively made by their male folk. This war coat is no more for practical use but still prepared in a very limited scale as a mark of their identity and specially used during festive days. This is traceable in a very few houses in a village today. The dress of their Shaman (*Igu*) is also unique and cannot be worn by any common person or women.

Food Habit

Besides maize, a red variety of rice, pulses, they gather or even hunt a large number of their food items from their surrounding forests in different seasons. Obviously, such items vary depending on the location of the Idus at different altitudes. For example, they use shoots (*Ichchu, Alo, Apa*), wild fruits (*Inoosi*, *Arubru, Deyapu, Aji Bru*), tubers (*Biri, Besa, Gena, Abiri, Matha, Aloka*), and rhizomes (*Sona, Soja, Soalo, Soabra*). They also produce a large variety of vegetables (*Ajinar, Arunar, Atonar, Akanar, Puchnar, Agronar, Abanar, Ekanar, Acluknar, Arukanar*), mushrooms (*Akupi, Akolo, Akueshambro, Akumeho, Akupu, Akrolor, Akuembraha*), wild peanuts (*Amuchi, Ekachi, Makachi*) etc. (Bhattacharjee , 1983).

Alo is prepared from a wild sago tree, which is very common among many tribes of Arunachal Pradesh. First, they peeled off the bark and then the stem is kept in water for some days, then taken out and crushed into a paste. Then it is baked in fire and taken as bread. Stem of this tree is also used as food for their pigs. However, it is famous as famine tree and it remains as prime source of food of the Sulungs of Arunachal Pradesh who remained dependent on the Nyishis as well as the Mijis to a great extent as their masters. It may be mentioned that eating meat or even chicken is taboo for Idu women but they are allowed to have fishes and different rats, squirrels, birds trapped inside the jungle. Naturally, Idus are expert in making indigenous traps not only for such birds, rats but also even for large preys, such as wild goat, boar, bear, etc. Such traps are locally known as *Bung, La, Shikhembra, Adrapo*, *Depra, Aku,* and *Atombra.* However, traps, which are used, for birds are called as *Aru-ruh, Poko, Pidi, Pe-ha, Chen-da* etc.

Similarly, for fishing, they use traps (*Tha, Pithu*) and net called *Etho* made of nettle fibers. They also use funnel shaped bamboo traps known as *Ayuku* for catching small fishes and harpoon type of spear known as *Angachoye* for striking big moving fishes. They use one kind of poison for both fishing as well as hunting animals, which are traceable only in the Snow Belt areas. However, killing tiger and monkey are taboo for them and any breach of such taboo needs lot of restriction for the whole villagers.

In Arunachal Pradesh, the Aptanis are known for their indigenous salt but Idus also made salt in olden days out of the salt licks of the animals (*Ahi*) from water which used to collect in a vessel and evaporated over fire which gave birth to small crystals of dirty brown colour which would eventually be collected having salty tastes (*ibid* : 71). Of course, most of their salt requirement was fulfilled through their trade with the plains of Assam, and even Tibet.

They also prepare a variety of local liquor made of millets, maize and rice, which is one of the most important part of their life irrespective of age and sex. Preparation of such variety of drinks involves their indigenously developed techniques, which remained with their female population largely.

Various varities of rice (*Keku*) like *Jijiko*, *Misenge*, (red rice) are used mainly to prepare the local liquor. For the preparation of rice-beer, at first rice is cleaned. After that, the rice is boiled and kept for sometime to be cooled. Then such boiled rice is nicely spread over the mat (*Arhrupra*) and one type of yeast (*Pa*), made of rice powder is sprinkled over that boiled rice. After that, the boiled rice is thoroughly mixed with the '*Pa*', which is added according to the required amount in relation to the quantity of rice available. Then the mixture is kept in a large basket (*Agra*) and after that, it is allowed to ferment for 4 to 5 days, which varies according to the seasons. In winter, it takes more time for fermentation. Whereas in summer, it takes less time. For drinking, the required amount of wine (boiled rice) is taken out of basket (*Agra*) and more water is added into it. Then only it is considered ready for drinking. The rice-beer is poured in the basket (*Yuru*) and the process of filtration is done. Again, the first filtered wine is re-poured in the '*Yuru*'.

The process of preparation of wine through *Yamba* (millets) is somewhat very similar to the rice-beer. Usually the difference is only that the *Yamba* is fried in vessel (*Kerai*) before boiling it. *Yamba* takes little long time to be boiled as compared to the rice beer. It can also be prepared along with rice (*Keku*). The process involved in it is same as the rice-beer.

The preparation of liquor made of maize (*Ambu*) also follows the same process as of rice-beer. First, it is dried in the sun, and then wetted for a night. After that grinding is done and the same process mentioned earlier is followed. It also takes sufficient time to be boiled.

Regarding the preparation of wine made or Tapioca (*Gedu*), firstly, the outer cover (skin) of Tapioca is removed and washed clearly through water. Then it is cut into small pieces and boiled, the fibers are thrown out after it is boiled. It is meshed nicely and makes good buds out of it. Then after it is cooled, '*Pa*' is added or sprinkled into the mixture or dub. It is kept in the basket (*Yuru*) for fermentation. Usually it is not prepared in a large scale.

The Idu Mishmis traditionally prefer '*Yu*' made of rice (*Keku*), millets (*Yamba*) and maize (*Ambu*). Nowadays, liquors made of banana, jackfruit and *papad* are also used. Usually these are not much preferred by them rather these are used as a substitute for the rice-beer. The taste of liquor also differs according to the variety of the items used for such preparation.

Preparation of Yeast *(Pa)*

Pa is made up of rice (*keku*) only. It is kept in water for one night. Then the wetted rice is spread over the *Epeye* (mat) which is dried in sun for few minutes. After that it is grinded nicely either by *Elobe* or any *Eprembo* (grinding stone). While doing so the wild leaves (*Ahupi*) is also grinded along with it. Then dub is made out of it and biscuit like '*Pa*' is kept in basket (*Ahonga*) by covering it with jute cloths. If the atmosphere is extreme hot, the cover of the basket is removed and if it is cool, then the basket is covered by more jute clothes. After 2 days the position of '*Pa*' is changed again to be kept for 4 to 5 days and only after that, it is transferred to another basket. It is found that if the wild leaves (*Ahupi*) are not ground when the rice is grinded, and then the biscuits of '*Pa*' are covered by the *Ahupi* leave for few hours.

Generally, an Idu keeps liquor (*Yu*) in the granary (*A-Ka*) whereas for the community's use; it is stored in the *Rehko*, the community hall where Reh is performed.

Food Preservation

The food items, like meats, fish and other eatables are kept in either house or granary. The baskets like *Atutu* and *Aproko* are used for keeping dried meats (rats, pigs, *mithuns*, deer's, other wild animals) and fish. The drying of meat and fishes is done by applying the process of *Akheta*, with the help of a stick made of bamboo, which is kept above the fireplace. Sometimes salt is sprinkled on the fresh (raw) meat and fish and kept above the fire rack, to avoid the loss of fats, decaying of meats and to avoid the attacks of insects (*Alupi*).

The roasted or smoked dried meat is consumed either directly or by boiling it with bamboo shoots. They practice salting, smoking and roasting methods for preservation of food items especially various meat and fishes. Such prepared items are kept in *Aka* for personal use but for community use, these are preserved or stored in *Rekho*.

They exchange the dried meats and fishes during auspicious occasions like marriage, Reh festival etc.

Table 7.3. Types of Yu

Name	*Contents*
Yu Yambo	Prepared from millet
Yu Ambo	Prepared from maize
Yu Keku	Prepared from rice
Yu Mazibanh	Prepared from banana
Yu Enjuphun	Prepared from jackfruit
Yu Eka	Prepared from *papad*

Ethno Medicinal Practices

Their traditional mode of treating diseases to a large extent is dependent on various plants and other locally available resources which their *Igu* used to provide to ailing persons besides their spiritual healing systems. Some of the names of such ethno medicinal plants and their use are given below:

Ethno medicinal plants of the Idus

AYAWE	Leaves are eaten in dysentery.
AJIMBO	Banana roots used for dysentery
AMBOKO	Grown in temperate regions. Bark is used against fever.
AME ATHRAL (Nettle)	Roots are against fever.
ALITA	Ginger like substances used for rituals in all sickness.
ATHRU	Plant used in dysentery.
ANOPOO	Used for stopping bleeding in minor cuts.
LIMUNA	Used for stopping bleeding in minor cuts.
ARMENA	Vegetable used for reducing joint pain.
LEPRA	Used for reducing joint pain.

Conclusions

The whole discourse reveals how Indigenous Knowledge System is linked with the day-to-day life of the Idus. It are true that like other tribes of Arunachal Pradesh, Idus is going through the process of transition. They have been exposed to various forces of change which have mostly effected their material life, even in interior village areas. Introduction of monetary economy as well as market gradually started replacing many of their utility goods, baskets, and even some of their foodstuffs. Undoubtedly new cultural innovations are moulding their daily life and at the same time replacing some of their knowledge base which perhaps is no more viable in the emerging new context. However, this study demonstrates how people tried to utilise their surrounding resources in a sustainable way on the basis of the knowledge which their forefathers must have accumulated on the trial and error method and passed on from one generation to another selflessly. In the contemporary context when 'globalisation' and 'liberalisation' became pass words for understanding changing human relations and social systems such textualisation of Indigenous Knowledge System may reaffirm the strength of knowledge base of the traditional societies those are still surviving in different parts of the world. However, with the emergence of Intellectual Property Right patenting regime, there is a great threat looming over, that is, unless we remain alert and make people conscious about such new policies and conceptual tools then our Indigenous Knowledge may also be sold in the international markets as one of the cheapest commodities.

References

Agrawal, A., 2002, "Indigenous Knowledge and the Politics of Classification", *International Social Science Journal*, 173, September issue.

Barua, T.K.M., 1960, *The Idu Mishmi*, Shillong: NEFA Administration.

Bhattacharjee, T., 1983, *Idus of Mathun and Dri Valley*, Shillong: Directorate of Research, Arunachal Pradesh.

Brouer, J., 2000, "Practices are not without Concepts: Reflections of the Use of Indigenous Knowledge in Artisan and Agricultural Projects in India", *Journal of Social Science*, 4, 1:1-19.

Dutta Chaudhuri, S., 1995, "Idu Mishmi", in P.Dutta and S.I.Ahmed (Eds) *People of India - Arunachal Pradesh*, Calcutta: Seagull Books.

Kalland, A., 2000, "Indigenous Knowledge: Prospects and Limitations", in Roy Ellen, Peter Parks and Alan Bicker (Eds): *Indigenous Environmental Knowledge and its Transformations : Critical Anthropological Perspectives.* Hardwood Academic Publishers: Canada.

Pulu, J., 1973, *Idu Phrase-Book*, Shillong: DIPR, NEFA Administration.

8

Indigenous Knowledge System in Health Care Among the Tawang Monpas of Arunachal Pradesh

Manish Sharma

India harbours a varied diversity of plants and animals and impressive variety of habitats and ecosystem. It has been observed through studies that "It is the treasure house from which future needs will be met with and where elements will be found that will form the basis of a new knowledge and technology". However, the environmental problem such as climatic changes, depleted resources, pollution, and undamaged and untrammelled use of the natural resources has enhanced the problems of habitants and ecosystem. Against this scenario, now it has been felt that environmental relationship must be symbiotic for sustainable development of the human society. After further analysis it has been observed that it is at the local level that both the wealth of diversity and threats to it are more tangible, hence importance of Indigenous Knowledge System emerges as an important issue.

Indigenous knowledge system means institutionalised form of indigenous knowledge of any society, which is transferred from generation to generation in a systematic and informal way. This knowledge is the outcome of hundred of years of researches, experiments, experiences and adaptation to local culture and environment. Indigenous knowledge covers a wide range of subjects such as agriculture, education, food preparation, small-scale industries, health care and many more aspects of life. Often indigenous knowledge system is looked against the modern knowledge system, but in actuality, both are complementary and supplementary to each other.

Importance of indigenous knowledge system is very well hidden in an African proverb, "when an old knowledgeable person dies a whole library dies". Due to less cost and readily availability, the importance of traditional medicine is much more in under developed countries. Indian Government has also realised it and has taken steps to create Traditional Knowledge Digital Library.

World Health Organisation has also felt the importance of it and recognise it by defining traditional medicine as "the sum total of all the knowledge and practice, whether explicable or not, used in diagnosis, prevention and elimination of physical, mental and social imbalances and relying exclusively on practical experience and observations, handed down from generation to generation whether verbally or in writing".

Major multinational pharmaceutical giants are turning to incorporate many of the traditional medicines into their product and are making efforts to access them directly or using modern tools of breeding and cultivation (tissue culture, cell culture, and transgenic technology). All these activities reveal the importance of traditional medicine.

Traditional medicine does not consist only of plants and herbs but many other things also such as animals organs, insects, flies, animal's products and spiritual activities (though spiritual activities are out of scope of the present chapter due to various limitations).

Under the new economic order of the world, particularly with the emergence of the WTO, a lot of discussions are on for Intellectual Property Rights raising issues like feasibility of protection of indigenous knowledge system with existing intellectual property right system. In this connection, World Intellectual Property Organisation (WIPO) held a conference in October 1998 and under the aegis of the WIPO, an agenda for the future of Intellectual Property Right in the field of traditional medicine was prepared, which patronise activities in this area, namely development of standards for the availability, scope and use of Intellectual Property Rights on traditional medicine in the Asian countries. The grant of patent for many known traditional medicine of the under developed countries to the developed countries is now causing a great concern to the developing countries. Now the developing countries rich in inheritance are feeling that they are getting or importing the same product at dearer prices what they were producing at cheaper cost by traditional method with the help of traditional knowledge. There are several examples of it, such as the patent registered for wound-healing properties of turmeric by United States which was challenged by India through CSIR to U.S Patent No 54015041 in 1997 and by COICA, an organisation of the tribal of Amazon region against US patent No 5751 in 1996 for B. Caapi a herbal plant.

All these examples signify the importance of indigenous knowledge system particularly in health care, where with less cost and easy availability of the medicine, people can get better health care facilities. Tawang of Arunachal Pradesh being a remote area with a treasure of huge biodiversity keeps much relevance for this type of study.

II

Tawang is the western most district of Arunachal Pradesh with 2,172 sq. km.. area of having 38,924 population and population density of the district is only 18 (2001 Census). The majority of population belongs to the Monpa tribe and the religion professed by them is the Buddhism of Mahayana sect. The Monpa of Tawang have their own age old style of traditional medicine, which includes the naturopathy, herbs in various forms (powder, leaf, oil, inhaling of vapour etc.), animal organs, birds and of course spiritual practices by the *lamas* and the shamans. They are simple and religious in nature.

Due to tough hill terrain with a range varying from 4,000 ft altitude to 13,500 ft altitude and cold weather they are subjected to cold prone disease. They use firewood to keep their living room warm. Added with poor ventilation facilities and no proper chimney for exhaustion of smoke, they are also prone to various respiratory diseases.

They use or practice traditional medicine for the minor diseases particularly the people living in inaccessible areas with scarce means of communication. Mostly the knowledge and information was passed from generation to generation. The specialty of this tribe is their social organisation or rural organic structure revolves around the monasteries and the Monks. They have expertise and are trained in selection, collection and processing, and the use of various parts of the herbs. During our survey, we found a lot of information about the practice of traditional medicine, which is shown in Table 8.1 in brief.

Table 8.1 : Lists of Plants and Animal Organs Used as Traditional Medicine

Disease / Ailments / Symptoms	*Local / Vernacular Name*	*Type of Medicine*	*Parts used*	*Mode of Application*
Eye infection	*Nyulum*	Herbal	Leaf, boiled in water	Wash
Mild fever, body ache etc	*Bashakaseng*	Herbal	Leaf, stems Fruits and roots	Swallow
Boils	*Chomcha*	Herbal	Leaf boiled in water	Drink
Dysentery	*Bashaka*	Herbal	Flower	Chew
Constipation	*Lhabho and Chuto*	Herbal	Flower	Chew
Sleeplessness	*Nyes*	Herbal	Flower	Chew
Weak mind and or Weak memory	*Yeers*	Herbal	Leaf	Take with water
Respiratory problem	*Chalum and Namlpa*	Herbal	Leaf	Take with water
Fever	*Chandoseng, Ohla,Chumi-ktang*	Herbal	Stems and Root	Chew
Cough, Cold	*Chandoseng*	Herbal	Stems and roots	Chew
Wound	*Chumiktang*	Herbal (Poison-ous)	Roots	Chew
During Pregnancy	*Chomeha*	Herbal	Stems and Roots	Chew

Disease / Ailm-ents / Symptoms	*Local / Vernacular Name*	*Type of Medicine*	*Parts used*	*Mode of Application*
Cut/Metal cut	*Glangseng and Damerapseng*	Herbal	Branches	Application in affected area after heating it
Burn	*Youngha*	Herbal	Stems and Roots	Application of powder
Constipation/ Indigestion	*Samerep, Komerep, Damerep*	Herbal	Fruits	Chew
Cough	*Ginger*	Herbal	Roots	Chew
Skin Problem	*Pine Gum*	Herbal (Cosmetic)	Gum	Application
Severe Pain	*Changseng+ Nyulum+ Poiye leaves*	Herbal	Leaves	Bath after boiling together
Cancer	*Jalapa*	Herbal	Flower	Chew
Respiratory track infection	*Chandusheng*	Herbal	Flower and leaf	Chew
Pain in limbs	*Shaaksheng*	Herbal	Leaf	Chew
Fracture	*Chapsheng*	Herbal	Leaf	Application of the leaf juice
Sinus	*Damrepsheng*	Herbal	Leaf	Application of the leaf juice
Itches	*Changsheng and thulasriful*	Herbal	Leaf	Application of the leaf juice
Measles	*Baigum*	Herbal	Flower	Chew
Small pox	*Chang*	Food product		Drink
Sleeplessness with headache and stomachache	*Dutpa*	Food product		
Fresh Bath	*Changseng*	Herbal (Cosmetic)	Leaf	Bath
Weakness	*Akmer, Sengmer*	Animal product	Ghee	Eat
Krackage of foot, lips etc	*Sengmer*	Animal product	Ghee	Eat
Stomach trouble	Liver of bear	Animal organ		Take after boiling it

Disease / Ailments / Symptoms	*Local / Vernacular Name*	*Type of Medicine*	*Parts used*	*Mode of Application*
Skin problem/Leprosy in initial stage	*Jushmangsha, Vamosha etc*	Animal organ		Take after boiling it
Fever	Heart of bear	Animal organ		Take after boiling it
Viral fever	Bile of snow bear	Animal organ		Take after boiling it
Liver problem	Bile of snow bear	Animal organ		Take after boiling it

Nowadays, the impact of modernisation is also seen in the villages in the health care sector. Therefore, this is the high time to discuss about it and popularise it among the mass.

Conclusion

There is a paucity of published literature providing information regarding traditional medicine in the Tawang district of Arunachal Pradesh. Considering the richness of the biodiversity of this region, this work is a small step towards the documentation of the traditional medicine. Government should take up initiative to take scientific researches to verify and testify the medicinal value of the traditional medicine. Today's patents regime can be utilised favourably in terms of economics if we make Traditional Knowledge System in general and traditional medicine in particular readily available to the majority of the people after its scientific verification.

Suggestion

The following points may be suggested to tap the Indigenous Knowledge System:

- Indigenous knowledge is still in an unutilised resource priorities should be given to utilise it properly.
- Intensive and extensive research practice should be adopted to give scientific base to popularise it.
- Proper documentation should be there right from micro level which disseminates Indigenous Knowledge System for preservation.

- Recognition by giving award etc. to the conserver of biodiversity and medicinal practitioner for their invaluable contribution.
- Priority should be given for the integration of Indigenous Knowledge System with science and technology.
- An organised body at micro level (at least district level) should be established to integrate widely scattered knowledge of medicine.
- Sustained effort on the modernisation of the traditional medicine should be given priority.
- There is a need to set up a Peoples Biodiversity Register, a programme to involve in document to protect their intellectual property right.
- Awareness programmes among the local people about the importance of traditional medicine should be implemented.

References

Bhattacharjee, S; K.C. Tiwari; R.S. Majumdar and A.K. Mishra, 1980, "Folklore Medicine from District Kamrup, Assam".*Bull. Medicos Ethnobot Res.* 1: 447-460.

Bhuyan, D.K., 1944, *Herbal Drugs Used by the Tribal People of Lohit District of Arunachal Pradesh for Abortion and Easy Delivery.* A Report Advances in Plant Sciences.

Nath, S.C. and D.N. Bordoloi, 1989, "Ethnobotanical Observation on Some Medicinal Folklore of Tirap district, Arunachal Pradesh". *Jr. Econ. Taxon. Bot.* 13, 2: 321-325.

9

Indigenous Knowledge of Plants of the Assamese in the Treatment of Women's Disease

Birinchi K. Medhi and *Mahaswetta Saikia*

Man's dependence on plant is as old as humanity. Civilisations of the world have been possible principally through the proper utilisation of plants through agriculture. Social scientists and botanists interested in the study of plants intend to find out various ways in which plants are related to the life of a particular community and the use of the plants in the surroundings in food, fabrics, household items, medicines, etc. From the remote past, plants have provided real and supposed means of healing. Every human society has developed methods and techniques to protect health and eliminate disease, in which plants play a key role. India has a pristine treasure of knowledge of the utilisation of medicinal plants in preventing and curing diseases.

Health is one of the principal asset of every human being. In different parts of the world, man devices numerous mechanisms for ensuring health and eliminating disease. The modern medical science, which developed in the West, did not create any obstacle in socio-cultural dimensions of the health because it is developed as a social science. Allopathic medicine became popular in the later part of the nineteenth century and from then it started causing flaccidity in the interest of socio-cultural importance of health. However, in recent years it has become a focal point of study by both medical and social scientists (Medhi, 1994).

Medicine made from plants has been helpful in preventing and curing human diseases since time immemorial. The Assamese people have a complicated system of ethno medicine handed over from ascending generation to descending generation principally through the process of socialisation. The Assamese ethno medicinal system has innumerable components like belief in malevolent spirits, black magic, breach of taboo, sorcery, spell, amulet etc., along with some medicines prepared from different materials including the various parts of plant. Effectiveness of some of those plant medicines are attested by the *Ayurvedic* system. The medicines prepared from plants play a vital role in the ethno medicinal system of the Assamese people.

Assam is situated in the northeastern part of India comprising an area of 78,438 sq.km. According to the *Economic Survey of Assam* (1998), during 1993-1994 there are 22,175,85 sq.km. land covered by forest. Forest of Assam is principally classified into three categories: evergreen, semi-evergreen, and deciduous and degraded scrub. Nature has endowed Assam with luxuriant floral treasure. Sarma (2001) writes, 'in no other parts of the world with comparable climatic, geomorphologic, and edaphically combination, such diversity of flora and fauna exists as they do in biogeographically limited area of the State of Assam'. A good number of medicinal plants grow wild in the forest of Assam, many of which are indispensably related to the Assamese ethno medicinal system.

Mangaldai town, the head quarter of Darrang district of Assam, is principally inhabited by the Assamese, Bengali and the Bihari people, each group is divided into the Hindus and the Muslims. A good number of villages hemmed Mangaldai town. The Assamese Hindus, Assamese Muslims, Bengali Hindus and the Bengali Muslims inhabit these fringe villages. Overwhelming population of the Assamese in and around Mangaldai town outnumbered the other population. According to Cantlie (1984), 'The term 'Assamese' is sometimes used to refer to those who are citizens of Assam; in this sense it includes tea garden labour and Mymensingh settlers. More generally, however it is used to denote the indigenous or long settled inhabitants who are recognised as Assamese, not only in language, but also in culture and way of life'.

Forest of Darrang district can be included in the evergreen and semi-evergreen types. Though plants sparsely cover Mangaldai town, its fringe villages are enveloped with domesticated and wild vegetations. The Assamese inhabitants of both the town and the fringe villages have elaborate knowledge of plant medicines and at the time of necessity, generally to cure minor ailments, they depend on that pristine knowledge.

Materials

The Assamese community living in and around Mangaldai town has age-old customs of using medicinal plants to cure women's diseases. The Assamese names of some of the ethno medico plants used by the Assamese people of Mangaldai area for the said purpose are given below in alphabetical sequences with English equivalents wherever possible, Botanical names, part of the plant used, and folk use.

1. *Anantamul / Dudhelata / Dudulilata / Naharpatia lata;* Botanical name: *Hemidesmus indicus*; Part used : Root; Folk use: Juice extracted from root is taken to cure leucorrhoea, menorrhagia, and syphilis; juice is applied to the affected area to cure syphilis.

2. *Anhat*; English name : Peepul; Botanical name : *Ficus religiosa*; Part used : Bark; Folk use : Bark is boiled in water and the fluid is allowed to percolate through a clean and thin fabric; female genitalia is washed with that fluid to cure gonorrhea, leucorrhoea, menorrhagia , syphilis, wound, etc.

3. *Asok*; English name: Rangan; Botanical name: *Saraca indica*; Part used : Bark and flower; Folk use: Bark is boiled in water and allowed to pass through a clean and thin fabric. The gathered fluid is taken to cure leucorrhoea, menorrhagia and stomach and waist pain created by those two diseases. Flower is eaten to regulate menstruation.

4. *Era*; English name: Castor; Botanical name: *Ricinus communis*; Part used : Leaf and root; Folk use: Juice extracted from leaves, root is taken, and paste of leaves is smeared over breast to stimulate the formation of breast milk.

5. *Amlakhi*; Botanical name: *Phyllanthus embelica*; Part used: Fruit; Folk use: Powder of dried fruit is applied at the mouth of uterus to cure excessive bleeding during menstruation.

6. *Bahka*; Botanical name : (i) *Adhatoda vasica* – which bears white flower, and (ii) *Evanthus indicum* – which bears red flower. Both the varieties are used to prepare medicine. Part used: Flower and leaf; Folk use: Juice extracted from flowers and leaves is taken to cure excessive bleeding during menstruation.

7. *Bel*; English name: Wood apple; Botanical name: *Aegle marmelos;* Part used: Leaf; Folk use: Juice extracted from leaves is taken to cure fever of parturient mother and puerperal diseases. It is also taken to minimise labour pain and for easy delivery.

8. *Bhedailata*; Botanical name: *Paderia scandens*; Part used: Leaf; Folk use : Juice extracted from leaves is taken to cure acidity, dysentery and body pain of the mother after birth of the baby.

9. *Bhomora*; Botanical name: *Terminalia belerica*; Part used: Fruit; Folk use : Powder of dried fruit is taken to cure different diseases of uterus.

10. *Bisalyakaranee*; Botanical name : *Menispermum cordifolium*; Part used : Leaf; Folk use : Juice extracted from leaves is taken to cure excessive bleeding during menstruation.

11. *Chalkunwari*; English name: Indian aloe; Botanical Name: Aloe *vera*; Part used : Whole plant except the root; Folk use : Juice extracted from the plant is taken to treat irregular menstruation.

12. *Chatiana*; English name: Devil tree; Botanical name: *Alstonia scholaris*; Part used : Bark; Folk use : Juice extracted from bark is taken to stimulate the formation of breast milk.

13. *Dalim*; English name: Pomegranate; Botanical name: *Punica grantam*; Part used: Root; Folk use: Juice extracted from root is taken to cure excessive bleeding during menstruation and to stop excessive bleeding during pregnancy.

14. *Dimaru*; English name : Fig; Botanical name : *Ficus glomerata*; Part used : Bark and fruit; Folk use : The bark is boiled in water and allowed to pass through a clean and thin cloth and genitalia is washed with that fluid to cure leucorrhoea; powder of dried fruit mixed with honey and sugar is taken to cure menorrhagia.

15. *Dubari*; English name : Dog grass; Botanical name : *Cyndon dactylon*; Part used : Whole plant; Folk use : If a girl does not attain puberty within a few years after crossing the expected age, a cake is taken by her prepared by the powder of the dried grass, mixed with rice flour and required water to overcome the situation.

16. *Ghanta jaba*; English name: China rose; Botanical name: *Hibiscus rosa-sinensis*; Part used: Flower and leaves; Folk use: Juice extracted from flowers and leaves in taken to cure excessive bleeding during menstruation, gonorrhea and to regulate delayed puberty.

17. *Garakhia tiyanh*; Botanical name: *Citrutus colocynthis*; Part used: Leaf and root; Folk use: Juice extracted from leaves is taken to cure glaring discharge during urination; paste of root is applied to the affected part to treat and relieves painful swelling of breast.

18. *Haladhi*; English name: Turmeric; Botanical name : *Curcuma domestica*; Part used : Rhizome; Folk use : Juice extracted from rhizome is taken by the mother to cure severe pain at abdomen after child birth, and to increase breast milk; paste of rhizome is applied to the affected part to treat boil in breast.

19. *Harghunucha / Harjora*; Botanical name : *Vitis quadrangularis*; Part used : Stem; Folk use : Juice extracted from stem or powder of dried stem is taken to treat irregularity of menstruation.

20. *Helachi*; Botanical name : *Enhydra fluctuans*; Part used: Leaf; Folk use : Juice extracted from leaves is taken to cure excessive bleeding during menstruation.

21. *Kapah*; English name : Cotton; Botanical name : *Gosypium herbaceum*; Part used : Bark and root; Folk use : Juice extracted from bark or root is mixed with water collected after washing rice is taken to cure leucorrhoea; juice extracted from root is taken to create and accelerate labour pain and to treat painful menstruation.

22. *Kanta bengena*; Botanical name : *Solanan kanthocarpum*; Part used : Leaf and root; Folk use : Juice extracted from leaves or root is taken to treat barrenness; if a woman does

not conceive in the usual manner, juice extracted from root is taken just after menstruation to generate the possibility of pregnancy.

23. *Kehraj* : Botanical name : *Eclipta alba hassk*; Part used: The whole plant; Folk use : Juice extracted from plant is taken to cure excessive bleeding during menstruation.

24. *Lewa*; Botanical name : *Myriopteron extensum*; Part used : Stalk; Folk use : A piece of stalk is inserted through the genitalia and kept there for three to six hours to cause abortion.

25. *Matikanthal*; English name: Pineapple; Botanical name: *Annanas sativa*; Part used: Leaf; Folk use: Juice extracted from tender leaves mixed with sugar candy is taken to cure continuous hiccup during pregnancy.

26. *Mula*; English name: Radish; Botanical name: *Raphanus sativa*; Part used: Root; Folk use: Juice extracted from root is taken to regulate menstruation.

27. *Olat kambal*; Botanical name : *Abroma augusta*; Part used : Bark and root; Folk use : Juice extracted from bark and root is taken to cure the enlargement of genitalia, irregularity of menstruation, disorder of uterus, leucorrhoea, and menorrhagia; it is also taken for well functioning of uterus.

28. *Purai*; English name: Indian spinach; Botanical name: *Basella rubra*; Part used: Leaf; Folk use: Juice extracted from leaves is taken to cure fever during pregnancy.

29. *Satmul*; Botanical name : *Asparagus recemosus*; Part used : Root; Folk use :Fresh or dry root is taken to increase the size of breast, burning sensation on hands and feet, continuous yawn, giddiness, sleeplessness, weakness after delivery, and to treat puerperal diseases.

30. *Silikha*; Botanical name: *Terminalia citrina*; Part used: Fruit; Folk use : Powder of dried fruit mixed with the powder of *Phyllanthus embelica (Amlakhi)*, and *Terminalia belerica (Bhomora)*, are soaked in water for a few hours and the fluid created thereof is allowed to pass through a clean and thin fabric. The gathered fluid is poured through genitalia to cure leucorrhoea; fluid is also taken to cure puerperal diseases.

31. *Syamalata / Saolata / Moulata*; English name : Indian sarsaparilla; Botanical name : *Hemidesmas indica*; Part used: Root; Folk use : Juice extracted from root is taken to cure leucorrhoea and menorrhagia.

32. *Tubuki lata / Tupuri lata*; Botanical name : *Stephania hermandifolia;* Part used : Leaf and root; Folk use : Juice extracted from leaves is mixed with the juice of turmeric rhizome is taken to overcome pain after abortion; paste of root is applied over naval and genitalia for expansion of genitalia to facilitate easy delivery.

Discussion

The study reveals that the Assamese people of Mangaldai area, both the Hindus and the Muslims, have immense knowledge of ethno medicinal plants to cure women's diseases. These plants are found wild in and around Mangaldai, some of which are carefully planted for future use. Women diseases like excessive bleeding and less bleeding during menstruation, leucorrhoea, menorrhagia, etc., can be easily detected by the diseased herself. However, the experts only can diagnose diseases like ill functioning of uterus, some of the puerperal diseases, etc. There are some folk medicine experts, both the males and the females, in the study area, who can diagnose such diseases. After diagnoses, the ailing person is treated through ethno medicines, the major ingredients of which are invariably plants. Sometimes the patient takes resort to modern physician and after detection of the disease take help from ethno medicine expert.

The diseases prevalent among the women of the study area are mainly related to the breast, genitalia, puberty, menstruation, pregnancy, delivery, etc. A good number of plants are used to cure leucorrhoea and menorrhagia. Abortion is practiced to avoid unwanted delivery. Stem of *Myriopteron extensum* of about 8 cm. in length is inserted through the genitalia and has to keep there for 3 to 6 hours or more. During the period, the patient should take complete bed rest. After abortion, usually the woman feels weak, which is compensated by taking juice of cotton plant's root added to the water collected after washing rice. The folk medicine experts of the area also informed that they could cure barrenness of a woman.

In this chapter though only some of the women's diseases are taken into account, the men experience the two diseases, gonorrhea and syphilis as well. Here those two diseases are included because the enlisted plants relevant to the treatment of gonorrhea and syphilis are usually used to treat the women only. According to the folk medicine experts, the female body is delicate in comparison to her male counterpart, and therefore, caution should be taken while certain plant is selected to prepare medicine for females. The plants used to treat the women are invariably used to treat the male patients, but not all plants used to treat the males are used for the females.

The people of Mangaldai area have expertise in selecting proper plant to cure a particular disease. However, they do not have the clear-cut idea on accuracy of doses and duration in relation to the age and physical condition of the patient. There are some instances of death of the parturient mothers during the process of abortion. Under the influence of modernisation, the ethno medical system has undergone conspicuous changes. New types of diseases have made its appearance, in which the pristine system fails to offer any remedy. The experience of the disease and treatment is culturally shared; similarly, the measure adopted works at cognate level.

References

Cantlie, A., 1984, *The Assamese*, London: Curzon Press Ltd.

Economic Survey of Assam, 1998, Guwahati, Government of Assam.

Medhi, B.K., 1994, "Health Culture in a Kaibartta Village". *Bulletin of the Department of Anthropology, Gauhati University*, 8: 39-45.

Sarma, K., 2001, "Forest", in A.K. Bhagabati, A.K. Bora and B.K. Kar (Eds) : *Geography of Assam,* New Delhi : Rajesh Publications.

10

Concept of Health, Disease and Remedy–A Case Study Among the Kaibartas of Assam

D. Dutta Das and *M. Dutta Talukdar*

It is a well-known fact that diseases have been creating problem to individual as well as every society. From time immemorial, all over the world people have been facing enormous sufferings due to some or other form of disease. Consequently, the man has developed methods of coping with diseases. Besides the advent of modern medicine, almost all societies of the world have the *emic* view regarding the disease and almost all societies have developed culture specific beliefs and practices regarding health and diseases. These culture specific beliefs and practices are not developed from modern medicines but it is indigenous medicines where from most of the modern medicine has developed. This type of indigenous or ethnic knowledge of medicine is known as ethno medicine. Ethno medicine is defined as the vast body of knowledge, which has resulted from the curiosity of anthropologist about the medical beliefs and practices of members of traditional societies (Foster and Anderson, 1978).

Nowadays the matters pertaining to sickness and treatment process have drawn the attention of social scientists because of direct relationship between health and cultural traditions (Sarkar, 1993; cited in Misra *et al.*, 2003). Traditional system of most rural population of the developing world finds patronage in urban areas as well (Kurup, 1977).

Consideration of ethno medical matters in the holistic investigation of the cultural life of communities is particular characteristic of the extensive community study research in Mexico and Guatemala (Chambers and Young, 1979; cited in Misra *et al.*, 2003). Ethno medicinal study fosters light on not only the indigenous medicine but also magico-religious belief and practices regarding disease.

Materials and Methods

Data for the present study was collected from the Kaibartas, a fishing community of Amaraguri village of Dibrugarh district, Assam, situated at a distance of $2^1/_2$ k.m. away from the Dibrugarh town. This village is situated at the bank of the mighty river Brahmaputra. They are pile dwellers because the water submerges the village in every rainy season of the year. They have their own culture and tradition which they preserve since long past. They are the followers of neo-Vaishnavism. Their economic pursuit consisted mainly of fishing. They are expert rowers also. They are short to medium stature people.

The Kaibartas of this village belief that some of the diseases are caused by supernatural powers. Through prayers and offerings, they try to get rid of such types of diseases. The people have their own indigenous methods of diagnostic and cure of diseases. Some herbs and leaves of wild plants are available in this village and are used by them as medicine. In this chapter, an attempt has been made to highlight some of the traditional knowledge system regarding the various kind of herbal plants used by them to cure the different kind of diseases, some believes related to diseases and also about medicine man.

The data were collected by various techniques such as interviews, case studies, and observation during the month of November-December 2003.

Disease and Indigenous Medicine

For some common type of ailment, the Kaibartas take resort to herbal medicine, which they prepare themselves from various plants, generally collected from their ecological settings. Some of the diseases and their indigenous methods of treatment are as follows:

(1) Fever (Jar)

Symptoms: Body temperature, perspiration, body ache, weakness and the patient does not like to eat or drink anything.

Therapy: Paste of *Dupar tenga* leaves (one kind of sour leaves) is applied over the forehead.

(2) Cough and Cold (*Sardi-Kah*)

Symptoms: The tendency of Nausea persists, cold, sneezing.

Therapy: The juice of black basil (*Tulsi*) leave, honey and paste of ginger is mixed and prescribed to eat three to four times a day. In case of babies, honey is extensively used for the purpose. The mixture should be lukewarm.

(3) Tonsillitis (*Dingir Bish*)

Symptoms: Soar throat and fever, difficulty in swallowing.

Therapy: Seeds of Soap nut (*Manisal*; *Satindes saponaiia*) are boiled with water. The foamy water mixed with a little bit of salt, advise gargle 3-4 times daily.

(4) Toothache and gum disorder (*Datar Bish*)

Symptoms: Unbearable pain in the teeth and inflammation of the gum.

Therapy: A paste is made from garlic, black pepper and arum (*Alocasia formicata*) rubbed on the cheek portion of the patient.

(5) Pneumonia

Symptoms: Dry cough, chest pain and fever.

Therapy: A paste is made from dry ginger (*Moran Ada*; *Zingiber officinale Rose*), *Pipoli* (*Piper longum Linn.*), *Jaiphal* (*Myristica fragrans Hout.*) and entrails of Porcupine and honey boiled with water is given to the patient regularly for 3-4 days.

(6) Body ache (*Gar Bish*)

Symptom: Pain of the whole body.

Therapy: The leaves of Indian privet (*Vitex negundo Linn.*) locally known as *posotia* are boiled with water and the patient is advised to take bath with this water.

(7) Jaundice

Symptoms: Urine colour becomes yellow, eye and the entire body becomes yellowish and growing weakness.

Therapy: Precaution is taken on the intake of diet. Oily and spicy food materials and meat is prohibited. Little amount of *Misiri* (sugar candy; *Sacenovum officinarum*) and 2 or 3 leaves of *Jetuka* (*Lawsonia alba Lamk.*) is put in to a glass of water overnight and the next morning the water is taken by the patient for 4/5 days.

(8) Infection of eye

Symptom: Pain in the eyes becomes red, difficulty in vision.

Therapy: Three Hibiscus flowers (*Hibiscus rosasainesis*) keep in a glass of cold water for the whole night and in the next morning this solution is dropped into the eyes. Eyes are also washed 2 – 3 times a day.

(9) Flaming of eyelids and pain (Aajina)

Symptom: Flaming of eyelids and pain.

Therapy: (a) Paste made out of stem of black arum (*Colocasia tesculenta Schott.*) is applied on the affected area, (b) The foam extracted from *'Kana Simalu'* (*Bombax malabaricum*) is applied in the affected area, (c) Patient is advised to touch the eyes only when necessary and wash his hands before and afterwards to prevent infection from spreading.

(10) Scabies (*Khajuati*)

Symptom: Itching.

Therapy: To get rid of itching the villagers take bath with hot water in which leaves of *Neem* (Margosa; *Azadiirachta indica*)were boiled.

(11) Stomach pain (*Petar Bish*)

Symptom: Pain in the stomach.

Therapy: (a) A thin layer of lime is applied around the navel portion of the stomach, (b) Mustard oil is poured on a betel leaf, heated and placed it on the stomach.

(12) Loose Motion (*Petar Asukh*)

Symptom: Loose motion for 5/6 times.

Therapy: Lemon (*Citrus paradisi Macf.*) pickle (made out only mixing with the salt) is advised to eat with hot boiled rice. The patient is also given boiled *Bhedailata* (Paederis *foetida Linn.*) and *Masundari* (*Ranunculus reniformis Walt.*) to eat with hot boiled rice. Ripe *Bel* (Wood apple ; *Aegle marmelos*) is also given to the patient with water and sugar.

(13) Worm (*Pelu or Kirmi*)

Symptoms: Itching around the anus, abdominal pain, weight loss.

Therapy: Patient is served to eat pineapple (*Ananus cosmosus*) regularly for few days. The twigs of *chirata* (*Swertia chirata ham.*) are soaked in the water overnight and the water is prescribed to drink in empty stomach in a few doses.

(14) Vomiting (*Bomi*)

Symptoms: Indigestion, dehydration.

Therapy: *Kalakhar* (a kind of alkali) which is prepared of burnt plantain tree, is applied on the head of the patient.

(15) Cut (*kota*)

Symptom: Incidence of cutting.

Therapy: A paste is prepared from ash of burnt cloth, coconut oil and tea, applied over the cut and tied around with a cloth.

(16) Burn (*Pura* or *Jala*)

Symptom: Incidence of burning.

Therapy: A paste of dry shell of turtle and coconut oil prepared and then applied over the burnt part of the body.

(17) Wound (*Gha*)

Symptoms: Infected area becomes red, swollen, hot and painful with pus.

Therapy: A pasts is prepared from small *manimuni* leaves (*Centella asiatica*) along with its root with little amount of water and then applied over the wound.

(18) Nose bleeding (*Ewa Bhanga*)

Symptoms: Nose bleeding can result from an injury to the

nose, an infection or when inner part of the nose dries up especially in hot days.

Therapy: Three leaves of bitter gourd plant (*Momordica charatia*) is crushed and 3-4 drops of juice is poured inside the nose.

(19) Conjunctivitis of baby (*Pheskurioa*)

Symptoms: Infection of eyes in which they itch and become red and emit a watery discharge.

Therapy: Breast milk of mother is applied on the eyes of the baby.

(20) Abscess (*Bih phura*)

Symptoms: A boil is an infection that forms sag of pus under the skin around it becomes red and hot, causes swollen lymph nodes and fever.

Therapy: Grounded leaves of Indian privet (*Pasatia*) are applied on the lymph.

(21) Polio (*Payalaga*)

Symptoms: Swollen bellies, thin arms, legs, and failure of a child to grow.

Therapy: The villagers believe that malnutrition child become cure if one cut a gourd (*Benincasa hispida)* into two pieces and mustard oil is poured in the mid portion of the gourd and this oil is smeared on the body of the child.

(22) Rat bite

Therapy: A paste prepared from betel leaves, mixed with smoky substance of fire and applied it on the affected area.

Some Beliefs and Practices Related to Disease

The villagers of Amaraguri are very religious in nature and they believe that if Almighty God is appeased properly they can get rid of many diseases. Hence, every family arranges at least a congregation in a year in the *namghar* (congregation hall of neo-Vaishnavite cult) for prayer. In that special day, the respective family offers various food items to God and the *raij* (congregation mass) and bows down to get *Ashirbad* (Good wishes).

Moreover, if a member of the family has been suffering from disease, then earthen lamp, incense sticks and *prasad* (pulse like *boot, moong* and fruits) are offered in the *namghar*.

As the people of the village believe that deity Bhagabati Aai (Mother Bhagabati) is responsible for pox, they offer *prasad* in the name of the mother Bhagabati.

The Kaibartas of the surveyed village believe that a man who has been suffering from body ache he or she will get relief if a man whose head come out last at the time of birth, message the body of that ill person.

Traditional Healer : Although the villagers have some knowledge about the ethno- medicinal therapy but there is a woman who generally prescribed medicine, which are prepared from locally available herbs and goods. The duration of treatment depends on the type of ailment as well as duration of ailment. According to traditional healer, the result of prescribed medicines depends on the stage of the ailment and on fulfillment of instruction given by her. Some medicines are accompanied with spell also. The healer usually does not charge but the people pay in cash or kind whatever they can.

Conclusion

The present chapter shows that the Kaibartas of Amaraguri village use various herbal remedies, some of which are found very effective for curing some diseases. The indigenous method of treatment is very popular among them, which has been passed on verbally from generation to generation. Even though the village stands at the portal of Dibrugarh town these people primarily, thrive on their traditional knowledge of treatment because of their undeterrable faith on these medicines. Their traditional treatment is based on their deep observation and belief in nature and environment. It is only when they fail to cure the patient, then the patient is taken to the allopathic doctor of the nearby town or Assam Medical College Hospital, Dibrugarh for treatment.

References

Foster, G. and B.G. Anderson, 1978, *Medical Anthropology*, New York: Willey.

Kurup, P.N.V., 1977, "The Science of Life (Ayurveda)". *World Health*. November 12.

Misra, P. and A.K. Kapoor., 2003, "Ethnomedical Practices in a Primitive Tribe", in V. Sahay and P.K. Singh (Eds): *Dimensions of Researches in Indian Anthropology*, Volume. I, Allahabad: Serial Publications.

Sharma, B., 2002, *Udbhid Gyanakosh,* Guwahati: Bani Mandir.

11

Indigenous Dyeing Technology of North East India

Dinesh Baishya

In India, the use of natural dyes for dyeing, painting and printing goes back into the prehistoric periods. The excavation of Harappan culture at Mohenjodaro revealed a cloth, which carries evidence of red dye. The excavated potteries of Harappan culture also reveal the use of dyes.

The decorations of the places and temples of mediaeval India, loudly testify to the mastery of Indian artisan in the use of natural dyes. The exquisitely coloured silk and muslin fabrics of India had acquired fame throughout the world during the sixteenth and seventeenth centuries.

Just how important were the natural dyes in the economic and cultural life of Indian people during the 17th and 19th century is illustrated by the uprising of Indigo planters of Champaran in Bihar. This rebellion also represents a watershed in the history of natural dyes in India.

The survey of the available literature revealed that there were as many as 500 plant species, which have been, identified as useful sources of dyes. Unfortunately, most available publications refer to less than 200 species only.

Being a tropical country, India is rich in equatorial and temperate flora. There is large number of fruit and crop plants, which are used as dyes. Some of the important fruit and crop plants used as dyes are pomegranate, mango, onion, safflower etc.

The use of secretions of three insects namely Cochineal, Kermes and Lacca (Lac) as dyes, are commonly referred to in this context.

The people of North Eastern region of India are experts in dyeing silk and cotton fibers. Even presently, in the days of influx of synthetic dyes, most of the tribes of the North East India are continuing the use of traditional natural dyes from plants for dyeing of both silk and cotton fibers and cloth. They use leaves, fruits, barks or whole of the plant for producing dyes.

From time immemorial, Assam has witnessed the manufacture of silk and cotton clothes. These clothes are dyed, and intricate designs with coloured threads are embroidered on them. Kautilya's *Arthashastra* mentions this kind of colourful embroidery prevalent in ancient Kamrupa. Adequate knowledge about the dyeing methods of ancient Kamrup was lacking. It was only after the advent of Ahoms, that the written records of this method were to be found. The local tribals have been using natural dyes to colour their fabrics. Till date, the Bodos, Karbis, Tiwas, Mishings and other tribes of Assam are using traditional dyes for dyeing clothes and threads.

It has been mentioned in *'Satsari Asom Buranji'* that when the Morans and Barahis of upper Assam came to pay taxes to Swargadeu Sukapha, they were elaborately attired in colourfully dyed clothes. The Ahom royalty and the officials used brightly coloured turbans. The dye was made out of a bright yellow coloured flower known as *kuhum* (safflower). Therefore, the turban was known as *'kuhum buliya pag'*. This age-old practice was prevalent until the early parts of 20th century in Assam. In the days of Ahom rule, a class of people cultivated this type of flower for its valuable use as a dye.

The dyers comprised a different class altogether, in early Assam, known as *rangali-dhoba.* In early Assam, the dyed threads were known as *anchu suta.* The name *anchu* is derived from a type of tree, which was originally extensively used as a source of dye.

Srimanta Sankar Deva, while in Barpeta district of Assam, had employed its local weavers to weave a piece of cloth, which was of a mammoth length. Colourful illustrations of the life of Shri Krishna were embroidered on this piece of cloth known as *Brindavani vastra.* This has been preserved in the Royal British Museum in London. The threads used on it were variously coloured and dyed by the local weavers, using traditional means.

The most popular colours used in Assam were red, light red, brick red, earthen red, blue, green, yellow, golden and bright yellow. Most of the tribal dyers of North Eastern India usually added country made alcohol on the dyes as a medium. However, non-tribal dyers of Brahmaputra valley did not follow this practice of adding alcohol. They use alkaline, acidic and alcoholic dye.

Alkaline dye was usually used on cotton clothes. Mulberry silk *(pat)* and *Muga*, were dyed with acidic dye. Bird's feathers and fur of various animals, bamboo and cane made materials were dyed with alcoholic dyes. Lime was also used as an ingredient in the dyeing process. The people of Assam also traditionally used certain chemicals and minerals in the dyeing process. *Tutia* (copper sulphate), *hirakhush* (ferrous sulphate), and *fitkiri* (alum) were some of the very important chemicals and minerals traditionally used in dyeing.

In order to create fast dyes, certain mordants were used. Some of the commonly used mordants are *Bhomrati* (*Symplocos spicata*), plants, and the leaves of *Barun* (*Crateva religiosa*) tree and the shell of *Bel* fruit (*Aegel marmelos*).

Plants used as Sources of Dyes in Assam

1. *Majathi* (*Rubia cordifolia*),
2. *Kusum* flower (*Carthemus tinctorius*),
3. *Achu* wood (*Morinda ngustifolia*),
4. Seeds of *Jarath* tree (*Bixa orellena*),
5. Barks of *Leteku* tree (*Bucauria sapida*),
6. Turmeric (*Curcuma longa*),
7. *Ranch* leaf,
8. *Madar* (*Erethrina indica*),
9. *Lochan* seed or *Gangai* (*Molantus philipiniensis*),
10. *Sewali* flower (*Nycanthes arborirstis*).

Plants used as Mordant in Red Dye

1. *Bhomrati* (*Symplocos spicata*),
2. Bark of *Khaira* tree (*Acacia catechu*),
3. Flower of white *Pama* tree (*Chuprasia tubularis*),
4. Flower of *Nahar* tree (*Musea ferrea*),
5. Leaves of *Bharali* tree,
6. *Bor thekera* (*Garninia pedenculata*).

Plants used for Yellow Dye

1. Turmeric (*Curcuma longa*),
2. Bark of *Kardai* tree (*Avarhoa carambola*),
3. *Kusum* flower (*Carthanus tinctorius*),
4. Roots of *Puli-Kait*,
5. Bark of *Tapor* tree (*Garcinia xanthochymus*),
6. *Kathal* wood (*Atrocarpus intigrifolia*),
7. Flower of *Palas* tree or flame of the forest (*Butea frondosa*).

Plants used as Mordant in Yellow Dye

1. Leaves of *Bhomrati* tree (*Sympolocus spicata*),
2. Tamarind (*Tamarindus indica*),
3. Peel of the seed of *Barun* tree (*Crateva religiosa*),
4. Flower of *Tita-champa* (*Michelia champaka*),
5. Flower of *Bogi-pama* tree (*Churprasia tubularis*),
6. Shell of *Bel* fruit (*Aegel marmelos*).

Plants used for Orange or Brick Red Dye

1. Bark of *Tapor* tree (*Garcinia xanthochymus*),
2. Wood of *Achu* tree (*Morinda angustifolia*),
3. Seeds of *Jarath* tree (*Bixa orellena*),
4. Shell of *Barun* seeds (*Crateva religiosa*),
5. Flower of *Nahar* tree (*Musea ferra*),
6. *Majathi* tree (*Rubia cordifolia*),

7. *Sewali* flower (*Nycanthes arbortristis*).

Plants used for Green Dye

1. Leaf of *Rom* tree (*Strobilanthes flacidifoliys*),
2. Bark of *Leteku* tree (*Buccaurea sapida*),
3. Turmeric (*Curcuma longa*),
4. Leaves of *Urahi-mah* (*Phoseolus lunatus*),
5. Shell of *Barun* seeds (*Crateva religiosa*).

Plants used as mordant of Green Dye

1. Bark of *Kordoi* tree (*Averhoa carambola*),
2. Fruits of *Bor-thekera* (*Garcinia pentakulata*),
3. Leaf of *Bhomrati* tree (*Sympolocus spicata*).

Plants used in Blue Dye

1. Leaf of *Rom* tree (*Strobilanthes flacidifoliys*),
2. Fruit of *Kordoi* (*Averhoa carambola*),
3. Shell of *Barun* seeds (*Crateva religiosa*).

Plants used in Black Dye

1. Leaf of *Rom* tree (*Strobilanthes flacidifoliys*),
2. *Xilikha* fruit (*Terminalia chubela*),
3. Bark of *Jamu* tree (*Eugenia jambulena*),
4. Bark of *Madhuri aam* (*Psidium guajava*),
5. Rind of Lemon fruit,
6. Seeds of *Bhola* tree,
7. Tender leaves and bark of *Dalim* (*Pomegranate*) fruit.

Plants used as Mordant of Black Dye

1. Burnt ashes of banana tree,
2. Leaf of *Bhomrati* (*Sympolocus spicata*), plant,
3. *Raghumala* (*Pothos scandens*).

Plants used in Brown Dye

1. Bark of *Amara* tree (*Amara rohituka*),
2. Seeds of *Bhomora* tree (*Terminelia belerica*),

3. *Kendu* fruits (*Dryospiros embryopterus*),
4. Bark of *Kharia* tree (*Acacia catechu*),
5. Leaf of *Dagal* tree,
6. Bark of *Siris,* Rain tree (*Albezzia lebeck*),
7. Bark of *Jamu* tree (*Eugenia jambolan*).

Plants used as Mordant of Brown Dye

1. Leaf of *Bhomrati* (*Sympolocus spicata*) tree,
2. Seeds of Barun (*Crateva religiosa*).

Dyeing Process

Red Colour : *Jarath* (*Bixa orellena*) plant is mainly used for red dye in Assam. Weavers or dyers collect seeds of *Jarath* (*Bixa orellena*) and preserve it for future use. The seeds of *Jarath* (*Bixa orellena*) usually are matured in the month of *Chaitra* (March-April). At the time of dyeing, the shells of the seeds are boiled to get a coloured decoction. The thread of fabric is then put in the coloured decoction for a long time. After the thread of the fabric is fully coloured, it is again soaked or boiled for fastness of the colour in a mordant. *Thekera* (*Garcinia pedanculata*) is used as mordant for silk threads and cloths, while *Bhomrati* (*Symplocos spicata*), and banana ash is used for cotton clothes.

Yellow colour: Roots of *Puli-kait* crushed and boiled with leaves of *Bhomrati* (*Symplocos spicata*), and cow's urine gives yellow dye. Besides, decoction of *Tapor* (*Garcinia xanthochymus*) boiled with leaves of *Bhomrati* (*Symplocos spicata*), mustard oil and bark of *Leteku* (*Buccaurea sapida*) is boiled together with threads of clothes for a long time to get a fast yellow dye.

Blue colour: Tender branches and leaves of *Rom* tree (*Strobillanthes flaccidifolius*) were allowed to ferment in an earthen pot for a few days. The liquid is filtered and boiled with leaves of *Bhomrati* (*Symplocos spicata*), to get a fast blue dye.

Black colour : Blue dye obtained from *Rom* (*Strobilanthes flacidifoliys*) tree is boiled with banana ash to get a fast black dye.

Traditional Dyes used by Tribes of North East India

Most of the tribes of North Eastern India dye clothes using traditional means until date. The Khasis, Garos, Karbis and many other tribes of Assam and Meghalaya are still using traditional dyes to colour their clothes. They use different types of dyes for dying of both silk and cotton fabrics. Traditionally dyed coloured clothes of these tribes are spectacularly brilliant and fast. Some of the sources of common traditional dyes and dying methods of some of the tribes of Assam, Arunachal Pradesh and Meghalaya are as follows:

Dyes of *Eri* Silk

Red colour on Eri silk: Eri silk is obtained from a kind of silkworm known as *Eri* silkworm (*Philosomia riccini*). The worm secretes the silk from its silk gland. The silk contains a kind of gum known as sericin, which causes difficulty during dyeing. Therefore, traditional dyers processed the silk to remove this material. The silk is boiled with traditional soap or soda to remove this gum material. The boiling treatment is continued for 30 minutes. It is then squeezed and washed thoroughly with cold water and finally dried. Only after completion of this process, the *Eri* silk is ready for dyeing.

To get a red colour, the *Eri* silk is dyed with the extract of lac and leaves of a tree, which is locally known as *Lynki* in Meghalaya. The lac is crushed to powder with the help of a wooden mortar and an iron pestle. When it is completely crushed, some boiling water is poured over the mortar and the material is mixed properly. Then, the major liquor is taken and poured into an earthen pot through a bamboo basket, which act as a traditional filter. This is done because the solution should not contain any grains of lac. After this, the leaves of the *Lynki* tree are cut into pieces. The yarn to be dyed is folded in layers and small pieces of leaves are placed in between the layers and boiled in an earthen pot with the lac solution. While boiling, care should be taken; that the yarns are not in the dye bath until all the water is evaporated. Some times, dying is repeated for two or three times to get a desired shade. The dying time ranges from three to four hours at a boiling temperature. After the yarn is properly dyed, it is removed from the earthen pot and dried in shade.

Yellow colour in Eri silk: To obtain a yellow colour, the *Eri* silk is dyed with the tuber of turmeric and the bark of a plant, which is locally known as *Dieng Rnong.* Before putting the yarn in the dying bath, the bark of the *Dieng Rnong* tree and the tuber of turmeric are crushed separately with the help of a mortar. A little amount of water is added to it and the material is filtered through a bamboo basket. A required amount of this solution is taken in the earthen pot. The traditional dyers know the amount required for a proper colour. The yarn is then put in the solution and boiled. The dyers also know the requisite time for boiling. Usually the duration of boiling is three or four hours, until the solution is almost exhausted. Of course, it is not to be left in the dye bath until all the water is evaporated.

Black colour in Eri silk: The *Eri* silk is coloured black with two materials – 1. A stone, locally known as *Eitnar,* and 2. A tree leaf locally known as *Sla Sohtung.*

The stone is first crushed to powder with the help of a mortar, and then warm water is added to it. This solution is filtered with the help of a bamboo basket. The leaves of *Sla Sohtung* tree are cut into small pieces. Then the silk yarn is put in the dye bath, folded in layers, where the leaves are put in between the layers. Then, the whole material in the earthen pot is boiled, until the dye solution is almost exhausted. This process of dyeing may continue up to four hours or the process may be repeated two or three times. After the yarn is properly dyed, it is removed from the dye bath, washed, squeezed and dried in shade.

Dyeing of Cotton Yarn

Dyeing with red colour : Cotton yarns are vegetable fibers. Cotton yarns also contain many impurities like pectin, nitrogen containing compounds, fats, waxes, inorganic matters etc. It also contains acquired impurities like dust, dirt, oil-stains, iron-stains, etc. To remove all these impurities, cotton yarns are washed with hot water and soap or washing soda. After a proper wash and drying, the cotton yarns are ready for dying. Dyeing process of cotton yarn for obtaining red colour is similar to the *Eri* silk. The raw materials are also the same, i.e. the lac and the *Lynki* leaves.

Yellow colour on cotton yarn: The material and methods of dyeing of cotton yarn are same as that of *Eri* silk.

Plants used as Dye by Khasis of Meghalaya

1. Dieng Rnong (Albizzia procerae) : This is a tall handsome sub-deciduous tree attaining over 80 ft in height. The colour of the bark is brown. The skin of the roots is yellow in colour. The root is specially used for dyeing red colour on cotton yarns.

2. Slapyng dong (Nelumbium speciogum) : This is a large aquatic plant with milky opaque creeping leaves. It grows wild in Khasi hills. The leaves provide blue colour on cotton yarn.

3. Soh Latarngei - Nahar in Assamese (Mesua ferra) : It is a very big and popularly known tree of both Assam and Meghalaya. It grows up to 200 ft in height. The Khasis use the roots and seeds of this plant as dye. It gives red colour in cotton yarns.

4. Musti : It is a perennial shrub about one foot tall. It is a wild shrub and bears small beautiful flowers. Some professional dyers cultivate this plant for dye. The leaves of this plant yield blue colour on *Eri* silk.

5. Sohkhu (Acacia concina) : This is a common perennial wild tree. It grows widely in the forest of Meghalaya, Assam, Nagaland and Arunachal Pradesh. The leaves and bark of this plant is used to dye yellow colour on silk.

Dyes used by the Tribes of Arunachal Pradesh

The art of spinning, weaving and dyeing is an important part in the life of the tribes of Arunachal Pradesh. It is the monopoly of the womenfolk of the State. Every mother, through her cradlesong, inspires her daughter to be an adept in this art. The colour, design and pattern of a homemade garment signify the age-old wisdom of a particular tribe.

The tribal weavers are simultaneously good dyers also. They have identified different plants for dying of cotton and silk clothes or fibers in different colours. The following are some of the important natural dyes used by the Apatanis, Nishings and Adis of Arunachal Pradesh.

1. Sankhii in Apatani (Symlocos paniculata) : Its leaves are boiled with the cotton yarn in water in an earthen pot imparting yellow colour.

2. Taming in Apatani, Tamin in Nishing and Gallo in Adi (Rubia cardifolia) : It is creeper. Small pieces of its stems are boiled with the cotton yarn, in water in an earthen pot, to yield red colour. Leaf of another plant, which is known as *Bukhu,* is added to the solution while boiling, and the colour becomes brilliant red.

3. Mubu (Apatani) : It is a tree, whose crushed leaves are boiled with the cotton yarn, in water in an earthen pot, to get a black colour.

4. Silop (Adi) : The bark of this tree when boiled with cotton yarn gives chocolate colour.

5. Sinking moling (Adi) : The roots and barks of this plant when boiled with cotton gives brilliant yellow colour.

6. Engot (Adi) : The leaves of this plant when boiled with cotton gives green colour.

7. Nimar (Adi) : The fruits of this tree when boiled with cotton gives green colour.

Conclusion

Natural dye is being extensively used for addition of values in handloom textiles. Researches have been done for standardisation of sources of natural dyes. New designs based on natural colours are being used for production of textile varieties. As the people of North East India were traditionally using natural sources of dyes, this knowledge may be used for development of textile industry in this part of the country.

References

Allen, B.C., 1906, *Assam District Gazetteers.* Vol- VI, VII, Shillong.

Bareh, H., 1967, *The History and Culture of the Khasi People.* Calcutta: Naba Mudran Pvt. Ltd.

Barpujari, H.K., 1990, *The Comprehensive History of Assam,* Volume III, Guwahati: Publication Board, Government of Assam.

Barua, B.K., 1951, *A Cultural History of Assam*, Guwahati: Lawers Book Stall.

Chaliha, P., 1998, *Purani Asomor Karikori Silpa,* Guwahati.

Chaudhury, P.C., 1959, *The History of Civilisation of the People of Assam to the 12th Century A.D.,* Guwahati. Department of Historical and Antiquarian Studies, Government of Assam.

Dasgupta, R., 1982, *Art of Mediaeval Assam.* New Delhi: Cosmo Publications.

Gait, E.A., 1926, *A History of Assam* - Report on the Progress of Historical Research in Assam, Calcutta.

Handique, B.C., 1959, *Purani Asomor Shilpa,* Guwahati.

Hunter, W., 1889, *A Statistical Account of Assam,* Vol-II, London: Trubner and Co.

Hutton, J.H., 1969, *The Angami Nagas,* London: Oxford University Press.

Neog, M., 1959, *The Art of Painting in Assam,* Guwahati.

Neog, M., 1965, *Sri Sri Sankardeva,* Guwahati.

Rajguru, S., 1988, *Medieval Assamese Society,* Nagaon, Assam.

Sarma, S.N., 1989, *A Socio-economic and Cultural History of Medieval Assam* (1200 AD – 1800 AD),Guwahati, Pratima Devi.

Trivedi, K.K., 1995, "Process of Dye Extraction in the 17th Century: A Study of Indigo". *Selected Papers in Congress on Traditional Sciences and Technologies of India,* Bombay.

12

Textile and Handloom Weaving– Some Observations

Indira Barua

Textile as fiber was acquainted with the primitive people when they settled with agricultural way of life. It is the human 'need' and the instinct for 'survival', which played a significant role in the development of culture and civilisation. In addition, in the growth of human civilisation, the introduction of weaving no doubt made a significant impact. The making of cloth is one of the most ancient of civilised craft. In the initial stage of human development, men met the demand of clothing in the minimal way, and the needs were fulfilled from the environment itself. Weaving has the potential for employment next to agriculture. With the introduction of an artificial dress material, the savage stage of evolution ends. Textile and textile designs of a people are an indication of the state of advancement in their material culture. Textiles are also a record of the historical, technological and mental development of the people who make them and for whom they are intended. Moreover, it is the field of textile and clothing, the cultural identity of a community is better displayed.

No one really knows for certain when men started weaving cloths. Probably, by trial and error method, it has developed into a full-fledged industry. Weaving as a craft developed independently in ancient China, India and Thailand in the far East; Mesopotamia and Babylon in the middle East; Greece and Rome in Europe; Egypt in Africa and Peru in South America. Weavers in those days knew how to extract natural fiber, i.e.

flax in Egypt, wool in Mesopotamia, cotton in India and ramie in Southeast Asia. Later on, the Chinese developed the art of producing cocoon from the silk worm and it was reeled into silk by a process knows an throwing. Along with development, considerable progress is made in the weaving industry. However, handloom weaving is by no means extinct, indeed, it is very flourishing and highly skilled craft activity followed in many parts of the world. India alone has still over 20, 00,000 handlooms at work. Cloths of the world-renowned quality of Harris tweeds are still made on handlooms of great age and simplicity. (Stowell, 2001, VII : 151).

In the present chapter, an attempt has been made to give a brief idea about the colourful textile and weaving processes and its socio-cultural significance in some communities of Assam.

Assam has a glorious cultural tradition in textile and handloom weaving. Handloom industry is the most important cottage industry in Assam. It has a tradition of woven textiles made from different materials using a variety of techniques for processing of materials for weaving and embellishing. Assam is also unique for its colourful tribes and communities and it has become a museum of races, being situated in one of the great migration routes of humankind. Each group is unique in dress pattern, colour combination and textile design. Thus, within the region, there are variations in styles of weaving, which have been retained because of distinct cultural traditions expressed through the people's ceremonials and rituals.

Among the diverse ethnic element, Tai is one of the significant ethnic element of Assam. Their culture display distinctive pattern in dress, food habits, house type, and so on. In Assam, there are two distinct classes of Tai groups, both belonging to Northern Shan tribes (Grierson, 1966). The first wave was that of the Ahoms, who entered Assam in the 12th century A.D. as conquerors and ruled for six hundred years (1228-1829 A.D.). The second consisted of five different groups who came into Assam at various times. They are Buddhist by religion. Though outwardly, it appears that the dress patterns of all the five Tai Buddhist groups are same, yet on a closer examination, it is also noticed that in some details these Tai groups differ from one another. So, in the present study, certain broad patterns of their textile have been described. Data were collected from some villages inhabited by Tai Ahom, Tai Khamyangs, Tai Phakiyals and Tai Turungs.

Assam enjoyed a high reputation for producing silk of fine texture. Eastern India (mostly the Himalayan foothill area) is considered as one of the most conspicuous mega-rich bio-diverse region of the world. The region harbours rich germ plasms of various silk producing worms and their host plant species unique in the world of Seri-culture. Silk weaving was mentioned about 2600 B.C. and earliest known Chinese textile is silk. It was being imported to Persia, Afghanistan and Mediterranean countries long before the dawn of history. Much interpretation has been made regarding the famous Assam-Burma silk route. Many of the scholars were of the opinion that silk weaving technique entered Assam following the migration of the Tai Ahoms along the Assam – Burma route via the Patkai. It was also referred that during the pre-Ahom period also rearing of silkworm and the people of Assam knew weaving (Gogoi, 1982).

Pat, muga and *eri* are the three different varieties of silk product of Assam. The colour of each variety depends on the kind of plants the cocoons are fed. Commercial silkworm (*Bombyx mori*) is mostly dependent on mulberry tree. The farmers do not possess regular cultivated host plant and they mostly depend on leaves of stray mulberry trees. Compared to advance States/Countries like Karnataka, Japan, Korea and China, no genuine efforts are made by the government to make sericulture a commercially viable industry. Seri-culture in the region is thriving more as a heritage than an economic pursuit unlike a modern viable industry.

The culture of *eri* worm (*Samia ricini*) rearing is almost a prerogative for the tribes of eastern region. Castor (*Ricinus communis*) is the primary feed for *eri* worm. The plant grows sporadically (mostly as weed) all over the countryside. The harvest serves only the family's annual need.

Muga silk has a natural golden colour and rare shining glow, which becomes more lustrous after every wash. "Assam silk, especially *muga* was very much in demand in Europe and it formed the staple trade of the East India Company during the 18th and 19th centuries" (Gait, 1967). Rearing of *muga* worm

(*Antheraca assama*) is mostly conducted in rural areas of upper Assam. The commercial broods are superior. The principal host plant for *muga* worm is reared outdoor, it is never considered as profitable for growers. Lots of care and precaution have to be taken for rearing *muga* worm. The operation is considered sacrosanct and superstition surrounds operations as the worm is taken as *Deologa* (possessed) insect. Though some researchers try to rear *muga* worm indoor on experimental basis, yet it does not show any encouraging result. As it cannot be produced in artificial conditions by controlling the temperature, the *muga* worm may be cultivated only in Assam. However, the saddest part is that due to industrial development and deforestation, the forest area with host plant (*som*) is decreasing day by day. The expansion of O.N.G.C. in Sibsagar area, (the home of host plant *som*) adversely affects the *muga* culture.

Another significant type of cloth is referred as *mejangkari*. The colour is almost like *muga* silk but slightly light in colour and finished product is soft. The costumes of the Ahom king were commonly prepared from such cloth. It is said that *muga* worm was reared in certain types of plants to produce this light coloured cloth commonly referred as *mejangkari*. However, even during that period, the process was not that easy, because worms died in slightest negligence and the host plants were very rare. Therefore, the product barely met the requirement of the king only. The above description indicates that silk of various types i.e., *pat, eri, muga, mejangkari* having different colour are produced by feeding different types of plants to the worms.

During earlier times, all the operations like rearing, reeling, weaving etc., were individualistic. No data on cost of production and expenditure on rearing plantation are maintained. It was mentioned by Major Jenkins, production of this stuff was carried on "in almost every village, but without capital, without division of labour by single individual, each of whom spins, weave and dyes his own web" (cited from Borpujari, 1996). The loom was in fact the center of domestic economy, the only hope of salvation in an hour of distress or despair. In course of time Central and State government have launched a number of measures for the development of handloom sector. Yet no significant impact is observed in Assam as compared to other States in India.

Human beings dress or decorate their bodies on a variety of reasons, the chief among them are status identification, real or imagined, self-beautification and magico-religious requirements. Clothes may serve to differentiate individuals or groups from one another on a basis of sex, age, occupation, rank and other social functions. "Individuals of different ages are recognised in all cultures by variations in dress, prescribed behaviour patterns and differential social status" (Piddington, 1963). Clothing's also serve to define ceremonial occasions, particularly those connected with religious rituals, marriage, mourning and social occasions. In the same way, only the people of certain rank may use certain colour. In Imperial Rome, "When a new emperor succeeded, he was said to be raised to purple because he wore a robe dyed with a purple dye so precious that it was forbidden for any other purpose. This 'Tyrian purple' was extracted from a Mediterranean shell-fish and was then made at Tyre, though there had been a dyeing centre in Crete as far back as 2000 B.C." (Stowell, 2001; III: 164). Colour also plays an important role in identifying an ethnic group. Every ethnic group guided by its cultural varieties chooses the colour of its own. Each group considered a certain colour or some particular colour as its exclusive possession, which no other group lay claim to. Most of the dyes are procured locally from herbs and trees. However, the chemistry and methods of the preparation vary from place to place as well as from tribe to tribe. The art of dyeing itself is very old and has been known for at least 4000 years. However, the dyestuffs industry as we know to day is only about 150 years old.

It has already been referred how the colours of *pat, muga, mejangkari* are produced by feeding different types of plants to the worms. In the same way different ethnic groups have their own way of preparing dye from herbs and trees. The types of trees and herbs used for the preparation of dyes are indigo plant (*Indigefera*), *Halodhi* (*Curuma longa*), *Sewali* (*Nyethanthes arbartristas*), *Palash* (*Butea frendosa*), *Juatic* (*Bixa-orellana*) and *Rum* (*Streblanthes flaceitifelius*).

The Buddhist Tais of Assam have their own distinctive designs, which differ both in making and design used by other people of North East India. Formerly, all the Tai women preferred black colour lower garment (*Pha-sin*). There is historical evidence that even the Tai Ahom women put on black coloured *Pha-sin*. Other colours favoured are yellow, dark blue, green and red. Designs were mostly combinations of green, indigo, blue, black and yellow played in horizontal lines, which were woven in their waist looms. The dress of elderly male is generally home woven chequered *lungi* commonly referred as *Pha-tung* or *Fa-tum* (*Fa*-cloth, *tum*-round). *Pha-tung* is usually made of cotton woven in checks with vertical and horizontal stripes. Normally, the *lungis* are green or black in colour lined with red, yellow, black, green, blue and violet strips. The *Pha-tung* worm by the Buddhist Tais of India is a borrowing from the Burmese because of latter domination over the minor Shan tribes in Burma. From the available literature also, it is revealed that Tais of Vietnam, Laos or even Shan do not use *Pha-tung* as the Indian Tais. Among the textile designs of the Tai people, the shoulder bag is very noticeable. The weaver expressed their great artistic skill in depicting designs of the shoulder bag. The bags are mostly woven in red and blue colours but design is woven in various colours. The imaginative skills of women reflect in flower motifs or flowers with trees, etc.

The Tai women knew the methods and ingredients of dyeing. For dyeing their cloths, they use a variety of herbs and creepers, which are available locally. Earlier, women used only the indigenous colours in their cloths. However, nowadays they prefer to buy coloured thread from the market. The investigation reveals that the women still know the techniques of dyeing and black colour is still processed by many.

A study among the Tai Khamyangs reveals that they have their own dyeing process. They use wild plant *Rum* (*Strebilarithes flaceidifelius*) to dye their *mekhela* in black colour. The plant *Rum* is about three feet in height and it is found in most of their kitchen gardens. First, leaves are removed from the branches and kept soaked in water until these are diluted. It requires three to four days to soften the leaves. Then alum is added in the solution and the mixture is stirred. After sometime, there appears sediment from which the clear liquid is separated. The sediments are then preserved in an earthen pot for about 15 days. The sediments are then mixed with *bor-thekera* (*Graciapedum-culata*), *modar mewa* (residue after preparation of indigenous alcohol), *kharoni* (ash of the banana leaves) and a little amount of black dye, which is kept preserved unused over the year. The cloth is kept dipped into it then placed in the sunlight for drying. This is repeated four to five times. The cloth is dipped repeatedly in a mixture of another liquid for permanency of the colour. When the whole process is analysed, it is revealed that it is a time consuming method. It also requires varieties of material in the dyeing process.

For preparing violet colour, barks of *Tumkao* (a kind of creeper) are collected in a pot and the thread like portion are removed from these barks. A little quantity of last years violet colour is poured into the pot and the decomposed barks produce a fine violet colour. For preparing yellow colour, barks of *Tepu* tree and leaves of *Ton Myot* (a kind of wild creeper) are boiled with water in a pot. A small quantity of yellow colour prepared earlier is mixed with it and thus a deep yellow colour is prepared.

At present, this indigenous knowledge of dye is not popular among the younger generation. A study among the Tai Khamyang revealed that "in the age group between 15 to 20 years and 21 to 25 years, there is not a single Khamyang woman with the knowledge of weaving and dyeing" (Barua and Das , 1997). It was also reported, "Till about 1950, the Tai Phake women used only the indigenous colours in their clothes. But in 1974, it was found that women folk preferred to buy the coloured yarn from the market" (Sharma Thakur, 1982). Such findings indicate that the traditional art of weaving and dyeing process is gradually diminishing due to various reasons. The non-availability of plant in the vicinity, time-consuming process and inter-community marriages are some of the factors which adversely affect the entire process. It is also a fact that, with the technological development, all over the world the synthetic dyes have almost entirely replaced natural dyes. Some of the synthetic dyes are the same as natural products except that they are made in factory, instead of being obtained from living matter. The best example is indigo, which was first synthesised in Germany about 1870 A.D. It took nearly 30 years of research and costs the firm, a million pounds to produce indigo commercially. If we look back into the history and development of human civilisation, it revealed that man acquires most of the knowledge from their natural surroundings, be it herbal medicine or natural dyes. However, with the ecological change and technological development, many of the indigenous knowledge system are on the verge of disappearing.

The study reveals that the North East India being a bio-diversity hot spot has tremendous wealth of plants and herbs. In the same way, diverse ethnic groups have a very rich tradition of weaving and textile pattern. Identity of an ethnic group is also determined by weaving and textile pattern. At present, along with the identity movement, there is a trend to revive the indigenous colourful textile and costumes. However, it is also a fact that the younger generations are not interested in learning weaving and dyeing at home. Instead, they prefer to buy the coloured thread or clothes for making their costumes. Moreover, many cultural items like Assamese *gamosa* or shawls of various tribes are manufactured at a much lesser price in various cities of India. Whereas, back home, they are hand woven and are not meant to be sold in bulk. So, effort should be made to popularise the colourful art. The entire North East India with their colourful tribes and communities having indigenous knowledge and natural resources may be considered as a cultural capital. It is urgently felt to find out certain suitable means to draw attention to the region's wealth of hand woven exclusively designed textile products and transform the area into a financial capital.

References

Barpujari, H.K., 1996, *Assam in the Days of the Company*. Shillong.: North-Eastern Hill University Publications.

Barua, I and B.Das., 1997, "Skilful Art of Weaving: A Study among the Tai Khamyangs", in K.C.Mahanta (Ed) : *People of the Himalayas : Ecology, Culture, Development and Change*. Delhi: K. R. Enterprise.

Gait, E., 1967, *A History of Assam*. Calcutta: Thacker Spink and Co.

Gogoi, L., 1982, *Assamese Sanskriti*. Jorhat: Bharati Prakash Pvt. Ltd.

Grierson, G.A., 1966, *Linguistic Survey of India*. Vol. II. Delhi: Motilal Banarsi Das.

Piddington, R., 1963, *An Introduction to Social Anthropology*. Vol. I and II. London: Oliver and Boyd.

Sharma Thakur, G.C., 1982, *The Tai Phakes of Assam*, New Delhi. : B.R. Publishing Co.

Stowell, G., 2001, *The Book of Knowledge*. Volume III and VII, London: The Waverley Book Company Ltd.

13

Textile Tradition Among the Tiwas of Assam

Sanjita Chetia

Handloom weaving as a folk art in Assam forms an indispensable aspect of the socio-cultural life of different ethnic groups. Assam is one of the major States in India where weaving at home has always been a way of life. In fact, the very socio-cultural life of different ethnic groups is revealed significantly in their textile produces traditionally. As the focus of this chapter is on the traditional textiles of Tiwas in the light of its socio-cultural and religious significance, it is deemed essential to understand the ethnographic context of Tiwas. Based largely on secondary sources of information an attempt is made to provide the ethnic cultural profile of the Tiwas whose textiles are discussed in this chapter.

The Tiwas also introduced as Lalungs are one of the plain tribal groups of Assam. *'Ti'* means water and *'Wa'* means superior. Again, *'La'* means water and *'Lung'* means rescued (Sharma Thakur, 1987). The Tiwas belong to the Bodo group of people, who migrated to Assam in the middle of the 17th century A.D. as stated Sharma Thakur *(ibid)*. Choudhury (1980) also reported that the Tiwas are the sections of great Bodo-Kachari group and during 13th or 14th century they lived somewhere near the Boro Kachari capital at Dimapur. Further, it is opined by Ghosh (1992) that the Tiwa tribe belongs to Mongoloid group of people speaking Tibeto Burman dialect of Bodo sub-group.

Concentration of Tiwas is mainly found in the Nagaon and Marigaon districts in central Assam. They inhabit in Kapili, Mayang, Bhurbandha, Kathiatali, Kampur Development Block areas of undivided Nowgong district and the Nartiang *Elaka* of Jaintia hills district of Meghalaya. Besides, there are a few Tiwa villages in Dhemaji, Titabar in Golaghat district and Sonapur in Kamrup district (Sharma Thakur, 1987). The total population of the Tiwas in Assam as per 2001 census is 1,70,622. As regards their religion, the Tiwas practice Hinduism.

Objective of the Study

The Tiwas have a very rich textile tradition with its ethnic characteristics and their contribution towards the overall textile tradition of Assam cannot be ignored. The socio-cultural dimensions of textiles of Tiwas have not been undertaken so far. Hence, a systematic scientific approach to have a comprehensive idea on the traditional textiles of Tiwas in the context of its socio-cultural significance is undertaken keeping in view the following objectives ; to study the textile tradition of Tiwas of Assam ; to identify the motifs and designs used in their textile ; to assess the status of textile in the socio-cultural life of the Tiwas ; and to suggest measures for preservation as well as improvement of their indigenous textile.

A village setting where the Tiwa people have been found concentrated was chosen for in-depth comprehensive investigation of their textile tradition. In selecting the representative village of the Tiwas, due attention was paid to the prevalence of distinctive traditions among them and the continuity of such traditions. The Tiwa village under Rangbang Development Block in Nagaon district and Kapili and Dalanghat Development Block in Marigaon district where Tiwas have been found concentrated were selected for the purpose of the study. The people of these villages are found to have preserved the traditional distinctiveness in socio-cultural and religious life of the Tiwa tribe.

Field investigation was done personally by interview and observation methods through specially designed interview schedules. Data were collected mainly from the weavers. The women in the village who are actively engaged in the textile production are only interviewed. The field data were supplemented by secondary information collected from various published and unpublished sources and analysed.

Textile Tradition of the Tiwas

In common with other communities of Assam, textile production is essentially a feminine craft among the Tiwas. It is customary for the girls to get themselves acquainted with the art of weaving from a very tender age. The tradition of unbroken continuity of weaving at home has played a vital role in making the indigenous weavers ever more skilled. Even today, a girl has to equip herself with various items of dress and other clothes to be used in her future married life. The weavers in Tiwa tribe use their indigenous throw shuttle loom. Cotton is the major raw material used for production of different textile items. In the olden days, silk textiles were also used in the indigenous textile and use of *eri* silk is however found in rare cases. In the subsequent paragraphs, an attempt has been made to give brief descriptions of the major textile items produced by the weavers among Tiwa tribe.

Kachang is the main item of traditional dress of Tiwa woman irrespective of their marital status. It is a thick cloth of 2 [illegible] x 1.4 mts. in size, woven out of 2/40 S dyed cotton. It is worn as a wrap around the body covering the breasts and reaching down near to ankle. The traditional *Kachang* is of black colour with yellow and green border. No particular designs were woven on this traditional type. Only prominent borders of 2 to 3" width, arranged in lines of contrast colours are used for its ornamentation.

Phachai is a piece of cloth of medium thickness traditionally used by the Tiwa women. It is tied firmly around the body beneath the armpits covering upper part of the body reaching down to the wrist. Two ends of *Phachai* are tied on the left shoulder. This particular textile item is woven out of 40 S cotton in the size of 90 x 30 cms approximately. The contemporary *Phachais* are generally found woven in black colour with ornamentation in red and yellow colour. Observation on two pieces of *Phachai* available at State Museum, Guwahati reveal that traditionally the *Phachai* was richly ornamented with geometric and naturalistic design having motifs like flowers, leaves, diamond etc. The *Phachai* is an important item of traditional bridal attire too. Although it was an indispensable part of dress of a married woman, due to availability of readymade blouse, use of *Phachai* in the present days is not found common. However, it is considered as an important item of traditional attire used in *Chagra* dance.

Thonali is a piece of thin cloth and an important item of both male and female dress. It is tied as a girdle at the waist over their dress. *Thonali* is woven out of 80 S cotton and generally white in colour. There is a difference in size of *thonali* used by men and women. The *Thonali* used by men is of 3.5 x 0.4 mts in size whereas the size is 1.5 x 0.5 mts in case of *thonali* used by women. It is interesting to note the difference between the *thonalis* used by the men and women in respect of design. The *thonali* used by men are richly ornamented with their traditional geometric design and structural designs at one end. On the other hand, the *thonali* used by women are ornamented with contrast coloured lined side border and designed cross border at two ends and small geometric motifs in the body of the cloth.

Jackai is a new introduction to the textile produced by the Tiwas. It is approximately of 6.25 x 1.2 mt in size, generally woven out of 2/80 S dyed cotton. No particular designs are woven on it. However, the border with lines in contrast colour is woven for its enrichment. Since, it is a new introduction to the textile tradition of Tiwas; it is worn only by the unmarried women of present generation. It is worn in such a manner that it alone serves the purposes of using *Kachang, Phachar,* and *Thonali.*

Kamcha is an item of traditional male dress of the Tiwas, worn in *dhoti* fashion to cover the lower part of the body from waist downwards. The *Kamcha* used for casual wear are generally cotton. The cotton *Kamcha* is either chequed or decorated with lines and of the size 2 x 0.8 mts. The *Kamchas* are also woven out of hand spun *muga* yarn in the size of approximately 5 x 1.2 mts. The *muga Kamchas* has its socio-cultural and religious significance among the Tiwas. The priest wears it during religious occasions, which is considered as indispensable in the attire used for *Chagra* dance.

Tangla is a sleeveless jacket of any required size used by men. They make it two side's seams leaving the armhole open. *Tangla* is generally woven out of coloured cotton yarn. Geometrical designs having diamonds, dots, lines etc arranged in contrasting colours are woven at centre front and centre back at chest level. A broader design with small geometric motifs is also worked at the bottom front and back. Fringes from just below the border designs are also made to enrich the garment.

Phaga is a loincloth akin to *gamocha* used by the non-tribal plains Assamese. It has multiple uses as men's loincloth, towel, etc. *Phaga* is woven out of 40 S, 60 S cotton and in the average size of 1.50 x 0.50 mts. It is generally woven white with the red and green as side and cross borders. Designs with geometric motifs are worked as both cross borders.

Phaguri is a thin cloth and an important item of male dress used as turban among the Tiwas. It has significant importance as an item of dress used in the *Chagra* dance. The priest also uses it. *Phaguri* is woven out of 60 S, 80 S cotton in 7.50 x 0.50 mts size. Traditionally it is of white colour with design at one end only, at a distance of 0.50 mts from the end. The design used in *Phaguri* is geometrical and arranged in different colours.

Cwalora is a piece of thick cotton cloth akin to scarf. Tiwa women use it as wrapper in winter. *Cwalora* is a handloom product of size 2 x 0.90 mts. Traditionally it is white colour with geometrical patterns woven all over the body of the cloth.

Japkapor is a thick cloth of hand-spun cotton of the size 2.25 x 0.60 mts. *Japkapor* is used as a wrapper by the male folk in the study community. This particular item is woven in plain weave pattern without any ornamentation on it.

Riha is an important item of married women's dress in different ceremonial occasions. *Riha* is used on the top of *Kachang* to cover the upper part of the body. The textile item is woven in plain weave with handspun *muga* and *pat* silk yarns. *Riha* is of size 3.25 x 0.75 mts with contrast coloured side borders. Floral motifs in red and green colour as cross border is woven as ornamentation of *Riha.*

Motifs and Design used in the Textiles of Tiwa

The ornamentation of the hand woven textiles of Tiwa is done in the loom itself. The traditional motifs and designs used in their textiles are found mostly geometrical and structural. Some of these designs (hand fan and serrated edge of saw) are found similar to that of the textiles of Bodo community of Assam. A few innovative designs, which can be categorised under naturalistic and stylised, are also observed in their contemporary textiles. Lines, stripes, bands and their arrangement in different contrast colours are found specific to their textiles.

An analysis of motifs and designs used in the textiles of Tiwa revealed that square, triangle, circle, diagonal lines, lines, diamond motif are used for enrichment of different indigenous textiles. It has been observed that the naturalistic motifs or designs like flowers, plants, animals, birds, etc were not used in the textiles of Tiwa until the recent past. However, the textiles produced in the present days are found ornamented with this naturalistic design in addition to their traditional geometrical designs.

Status of Textiles in the Socio-cultural life of the Tiwas

The Tiwa, as already mentioned, are still preserving the traditional traits of their socio-cultural life to a considerable extent. Handloom weaving among Tiwas continues as a living art and considered as indispensable in their socio-economic and cultural life. The womenfolk, specially the grown up girls are deeply attached to their looms and devote their attention to handloom weaving in their leisure hours. They weave almost all the required cloths for themselves and for other members of the family.

It was customary among all the indigenous communities of Assam for the bride to weave the wedding attire herself and to some extent for the bridegroom too. Though this tradition is gradually disappearing from the caste Assamese culture, it is still in existence among the Tiwas as in case of tribal culture both in the plains and hills. Use of culture specific traditional dress among different groups in Assam plays an important role in the textile tradition of respective communities. The Tiwas put on the dresses having their distinct cultural connotation for their general wear especially in wedding, death and other religious ceremonies and festivals. On the other hand, the distinctive item of dresses of Tiwas, particularly of women folk are not readily available in the market since commercial production is yet to commence. Such circumstances have kept the tradition of textile production alive among the Tiwas.

The Tiwas consider their textile items having characteristic geometric motifs like diamond shaped dots, triangles, square, circle, diamond within diamond etc., as indigenous to them as well as symbol of cultural identity. The designs as hand fan and serrated edge of saw, mostly used in *thonali* (a girdle) are never used in the textile items used to cover the lower part of the body.

It is interesting to note the socio-cultural forces lie behind the continuity of textile traditions among Tiwas. The *Muga Kamchas* (*dhoti*) has its socio-cultural and religious significance among the Tiwas. The priest wears it in religious occasion, which is considered indispensable in the attire used for *Chagra* dance.

It is evident from the discussion that these are important elements of continuity in the weaving traditions among Tiwas. However, many changes have been incorporated in the aspect of material culture largely due to the impact of external factors. These changes in the use of raw materials have been noted, in the use of motifs and designs from symbolic to innovative and vivid patterns. The women still prefer to weave in their age-old indigenous looms with low productivity and high cost production in terms of time and labour.

Conclusion

The indigenous textile items play an important role as symbolic elements in the projection of cultural identity. Growing cultural awareness induces the Tiwa people to dress in their traditional ways using culturally prescribed items of dress, especially on ceremonial and religious occasions. Such cultural awareness has certainly aided towards revival and continuance of indigenous textile tradition.

The study revealed that the indigenous weavers in Tiwa tribe need to be encouraged and inspired through proper technical guidance, financial aid, organisational backing for marketing, etc., keeping in view the development of handloom weaving of the study tribe. Such measures would help the indigenous weavers to develop further their skill in weaving. This would also inspire the weavers to continue the craft of weaving not only for keeping alive a valuable tradition but also as a commercial proposition and thereby enhance the socio-economic status of Tiwa weavers of Assam.

References

Choudhury, M. M., 1980, *Tribes of Assam Plains*. Guwahati: Directorate of Welfare of Plains Tribes and Backward Classes, Assam.

Ghosh, G. K., 1992, *Tribals and Their Culture*, Volume 1.

Sharma Thakur, G. C.; B. N. Bordoloi and M. C. Saikia, 1987, *Tribes of Assam*, Guwahati: Tribal Research Institute, Assam.

14

Traditional System of Seed and Food Storage Among the Tengaponiya Deoris– A Case Study

Sudakshina Das

Deoris are a prominent ethnic group of Assam. They are chiefly distributed in Sibsagar, Dibrugarh, Tinsukia, Shonitpur and Lakhimpur districts of upper Assam. Deoris are comprised of three distinct sub-groups, Borgonya, Dibongiya and Tengaponiya. Another group Patorgonya said to exist in the earlier days according to myths prevalent among Deoris, are not traceable now.

Tengaponiya Deoris have acquired their name from 'Tengapani' river of Sibsagar district. At present, they are found in Sibsagar, Dibrugarh, Tinsukia and Lakhimpur districts.

The main habitat of Tengaponiya Deoris is Kalowlowa Deori Gaon, Ranapur Deori Gaon, Udaipur Deori Gaon, and Madhupur Deori Gaon in Dibrugarh District. In Sibsagar district, they are found in Tengaponia Deori Gaon, and Ghelgheli Deori Gaon, whereas in Tinsukia District, they are concentrated in Mahadevpur Deori Gaon (Sadiya).

Like all other Deori sub-group, the Tengaponiya Deoris too depend upon agriculture. Their fields are within the territory of their own village. The villages are self-sufficient showing subsistence economic system. They produce and use the things required to meet the bare necessities of life.

The specialty of Deoris as agriculturist is that they produce all types of essential stuff like rice, pulse, cereals, vegetables, oil seed, tuber and bulb, crops and spices in their own field.

The common agricultural crops produced by Deoris to meet the demand of essential foodstuffs are:

Carbohydrate

(a) Rice is the staple food. Many local varieties along with modern crossed varieties.

(b) Potato: All indigenous varieties (small sized potato, *mua alo*, sweet potato) and available modern varieties.

(c) Colocacia spp: All indigenous varieties.

(d) Cereals : Maize (local varieties).

Protein

(a) Pulse : Black gram and occasionally *Arahar.*

(b) Fish and Meat : from livestock rearing and fishing.

Lipids

Oil seeds : mainly mustard and occasionally sesame.

Vitamins and minerals

Vegetables and fruits : All types of common vegetables, herbs and like many leafy vegetables, cabbage, cauliflower, brinjal, bottle gourd, bitter gourd, ridged gourd, cucumber, pumpkin, beans, etc. Local fruits like mango, jackfruits, pineapples, custard apples etc., and many indigenous fruits like *leteku, paniyal* etc.

Spices : Turmeric, ginger, black pepper, chilli, onion, and garlic.

They store these food crops (except vegetable and fruits) and seeds for the next cropping season. However, due to high rainfall and high humid condition of upper Brahmaputra valley, storage is a problem. The stored grain and other products are subjected to the attacks of insects, rats, birds and micro-organisms. Among them, birds cause damage in field, thrashing yard and in open storage. Considerable damage in internal storage are done by insects, rats and microorganisms like fungi, bacteria etc. Some of the important storage parts are recorded hereunder.

Material and Methods

The present study is based on a qualitative survey at Madhupur Deori Gaon. Survey sites and people are selected randomly. Knowledge is gathered by simple observation and by interviewing men and women farmers of different age groups.

Group of Organism	*Common Name*	*Scientific Name*
Insects	Rice weevil	*Sitophilusa oryzae*
	Rice moth	*Corcyra cephalonica*
	Lesser grain borer	*Rhizopertha dominica*
	Pulse beetle	*Callosobruchus hinen*
Rodents	House mouse	*Mus musculus*
	House rat, black rat	*Rattus rattus*
	Brown rat	*Rattus norvegicus*
	Indian mole rat	*Bandicota bengalensis*
	Large bandicoot	*Bandicoota indica*
Birds	House crow	*Corvus spendens*
	House sparrow	*Passer domesticus*
	Common mynah	*Acridotherus tritis*
	Common pigeon	*Columba livia*
	Rose ringed parakeet	*Psittacula krameri*
Micro-organisms	Fungi	*Aspergillus spp*
		Penicilium sp
		Sporendonema spp
	Bacteria	*Pseudomonous spp*
		Salmonella spp
	Yeast	*Monilia sp*
		Cadida sp
		Fusidium sp
	Actinomycetis	*Actinomyceties allida*
		A. graminis
		A. globisporus

Observation

The storage method practiced by the Tengaponiya Deoris is very simple but very different. The system is eco-friendly and free from health hazards. There are two main storage structures - *Bhoral* (storage of grains) and *Tipai Hal* or *Juhal* (hearth).

Bhoral : The main storage for rice is called as *Bhoral*. It is a rectangular structure made of bamboo and the roof is covered with hay. The *Bhoral* is placed on high post so that the floodwater cannot cause any harm to stored grain during rainy season. *Bhoral* is located in airy and sunny open placc in front of the house generally. Sunlight and air can easily pass through the bamboo walls of *Bhoral*. The staircase of the *Bhoral* is narrow one made of wood, tree trunk or bamboo ladder. The narrow structure of the staircase prevents easy entry of anyone so that the *Bhoral* remain free of germs and micro-organisms carried by human being. This structure is ideal for rice storage in warm and high humid conditions of upper Assam. At one side of the *Bhoral* there is an extension with open sides to store hay stack. The hay is chiefly used as fodder during rainy season. The adjacent courtyard of the *Bhoral* is used for different domestic purposes, chiefly as husking and threshing ground. The size and number of the *Bhoral* depends upon the economic status of the farmer. The Tengaponiya Deori does not use any kind of herb inside the *Bhoral.*

Tipai Hal or *Juhal* means hearth. Two hearths are generally found in each household, one is used for cooking and second one is used for sitting purpose of family and guests. Both the hearths are used as storage site with particular structure. The houses of Deori generally rest on high posts and called as *Chang ghar*. This is an indigenous style of housing suitable for flood plain upper Assam. The floor is generally made of wood or bamboo. Over this floor hearths are made of a square platform measuring about 4 – 5 square feet in size, made of high quality timber. The wooden platform is polished with mud so that fire of the hearth cannot burn up the wooden platform.

Over this platform, fire is lit up with dry wooden pieces

(called as *Khori)*. There are two or three hanging platforms found. These hanging platforms are made of bamboo and usually called as *Chang* or *Dhowachang* in Assamese language. Among the Tengaponiya Deoris, the upper most bamboo shelf over the hearth which is adjacent to the roof of the kitchen is called as *Lueng*. It is generally rectangular. This shelf is used for storage purpose of potato, onion and garlic. Some vegetables like pumpkin, peer gourd, etc. are stored in this *Lueng* and used until the crops of next are matured.

The second hanging shelf over the hearths is *Gisong*. It is square shaped made of thinly woven bamboo sticks. This *Gisong* is used for storing of dry fish in bamboo structure called as *Chunga*. Meats are also occasionally stored for a very short period. The *Gisong* is used to store seeds of different vegetables. Some vegetables are preserved as a whole for seed purpose in full ripe condition. For example, ridged gourd. In some vegetables, seeds are separated and tied up in cotton cloths and placed over the *Gisong*. Earthen pots are also used to store seeds and placed over *Gisong*.

During the rainy season, when fishes are available in large numbers, people collect fishes from local streams, ponds and wetlands. Such a large quantity of fish cannot be consumed at the same time. The remaining quantity of the fishes are cleaned and dried in the third temporary shelf known as *Chaloni* made of bamboo. This *Chaloni* is not a permanent feature like *Lueng* and *Gisong*.

Storing methods of different foodstuffs

Type of Food	*Stuff Source*	*Method of Storage and Preservation*
Carbohydrate	Rice	Stored in *Bhoral* located in sunny and airy area.
	Tuber crops	Placed scantily over the *Lueng*, which is airy and dry due to the presence of heat and smoke.
	Cereals	Preserved in cans with tight lids or in earthen pots whose mouth is tied up with a piece of cotton cloth and properly placed over *Lueng* or *Gisong*.
	Protein	Fish: At first the local fishes are thoroughly cleaned and dried up on a

		Chaloni over the hearth. The heat of the fire from hearth dehydrates the fishes, which are then placed in bamboo pots called as *Chunga*. The fishes are mixed with colocasia plants. This plant is a rich source of iodine and iron. Therefore, the whole preservation method produces a very nutritious food. The mouth of the *Chunga* is closed with local herb called *Bihlongoni*, which acts as herbal pesticides.
	Meat	Meats are rarely preserved for a very short period in earthen pots placed over *Lueng* and *Gisong*.
	Pulses	Black grams are produced in adequate quantity stored up to next season. Black grams are threshed thoroughly and the pulse portion only kept in pots or gunny bags. Fungus and bacteria generally infect pulses during rainy season. So the villagers put the pulses in gunny bags, sew the open ends. Then place the gunny bags at the doors and used as a door mat, that is each and every person goes over the gunny bags which contains the black grams. The airy disturbances caused by the people prevent from the infestation of the micro-organisms in black grams. Often the plant parts of the black grams after threshing are burnt. The ashes produced may be preserved separately and some part of the ashes mixed with black grams in gunny bags, so that pest cannot attack the grams easily.
	Lipid	Oil seeds: Mostly mustard seeds preserved in earthen pot, the mouth tied with cotton cloth kept in the kitchen.
Carbohydrate with Vitamins and Minerals	Vegetables	Most of the vegetables are perishable and used seasonally. Only vegetables like pumpkins (*Kumura*) can be

		preserved for almost one year when placed over the *Lueng*.
	Fruits	Ripe fruits are not preserved in traditional ways. Raw fruits may be preserved as pickle.
Spices	Turmeric	Preserved as powder in bottles. However, a sizeable portion of the crops are preserved in shallow pits in shadowy area. This process helps to retain the juice of the turmeric.
	Ginger	Gingers are preserved in shallow pits of shadowy place to retain the juicy nature.
	Onion	Onions are preserved over *Lueng*.
	Garlic	The bulb crop is preserved along with the plant, which is 8 to 10 inches in length, protects the garlic from the attacks of the micro-organisms, which infest the garlic from the tip. The garlic is also preserved over the *Lueng*.
	Black pepper	Black peppers are gently boiled or washed with boiling water and then dried in sun. After that, black peppers are tied with cotton cloth and placed on *Gisong*.
	Khar or Alkali	It is a very special food products of Assam. Tengaponiya Deoris prepares this *Khar* by burning the plant part of black gram. The ashes after burning preserved in dry bottle gourd. They used dry *Bihlongoni*, a local herbs, to close the opening of the bottle gourds.

Analysis of seeds sorting methods

Materials	*Methods of storage and preservation*
Rice	The healthy, high yielding rice strains are preserved carefully in *Bharal* in such a way that the farmers can easily identify the particular strains to produce seedlings for next year cropping. To grow up the seedlings, the farmers put the rice seeds of best variety in specialised bamboo structures called *Tom*.

Black Grams	Black gram seeds are preserved in gunny bags.
Oil seeds	Oil seeds are preserved in earthen pots or air tight containers.
Vegetables	Some vegetables (for example ridge gourd), which are well ripe, are preserved with whole body placed over or near *Gisong*. However, seeds of many vegetables like bitter gourds, cucumber, ladies finger, pumpkin etc are washed and tied with cotton cloths and then placed over *Gisong*. The heat of the hearth gradually dehydrates the cell sap. The heat and the smoke of the hearth also keep away the different pests and protect the seeds from browning caused by fungus infection. Potatoes are preserved over the *Lueng*.
Spices	Turmeric and ginger are preserved in shallow pits and remain covered by humid soil. The water or juicy content of the ginger and turmeric should be retainedfor germination. Garlic and onion are placed over *Lueng*, and are used for both food, and seed purpose.

Discussion

As we have gone through the different storage structures and storage methods, one thing becomes very clear that these facts revealed a good kind of indigenous knowledge about storage and preservation. The whole practice is very organic. It is not only organic in the sense that they do not use chemical pesticides, but also from the point, entire system is specially adapted with surrounding environment. Though chemical pesticides with their severe poisonous side effects are mostly banned in the western countries, they are in much use by our people – due to ignorance. Illiteracy is one of the major causes. Some persons used these chemicals with their full knowledge for commercial gains only. In such a situation, we should again look back to the indigenous knowledge practiced by different ethnic groups of our country. These age old methods of storage and preservation may not be useful for commercial gain. Nevertheless, it is time proven that they will not create health hazards. The knowledge is eco-friendly and can be incorporates into the integrated pest management system. Such indigenous technical knowledge not only saves our health, it saves the eco-system from pollution, saves the earth and our future generation.

15

Folk Wisdom of the Boros as Reflected in their Literature

Junu Mahanta

Human race since its origin had to engage constantly to tame the hostile forces of nature in making their life smooth and wholesome in this world. This happens to be continuous process for long and they learnt many things that have great practical values. Thus, the knowledge they gathered in their continual struggle for existence, for daily bread and for survival of their lineage is retained and transmitted to their fellow beings and offspring's. Finally with the considerable development of their life and society these knowledge acquired from varied experiences of their failure and success have been emerged as folk literature which eventually proves to be the greatest store house of all knowledge of the primitive society of the mankind.

The songs and sayings, adages, tales and myths tell us a great deal about behaviour, knowledge, appreciation and attitude of all the communities towards the object of the outer world. This knowledge is not the result of any scientific observation or experiment. Instead, these results of true experience are gathered in course of their rough and hazardous journey that had to be traversed in their way of survival.

All human societies possess folklore, which is the spontaneous and autochthonous creation of unsophisticated, simple, unlettered folk, and they are the storehouse of accumulated wisdom that acts as a guide for the people belonging to the same tribe. Originally, though it was a product of a particular individual, it came to be recognised as the group product. Studying and realizing their practical values, Malinowski, the reputed anthropologists, remarks, "Tales and myths are an extremely important element in the culture of an isolated island group. They are much more than entertainment; they are a part of the primitive men's science, medicine, religion, law and agriculture" (cited from Thompson, 1946). Therefore, an anthropologist studying a given phenomenon of a culture usually uses folklore data as supportive evidence to satisfy his conclusion.

In view of this perspective, an endeavour is made in this chapter to show how the knowledge and attitude towards life of the Boros is revealed in their folk literature. Of course, the study, in this chapter, will be a general one and neither of any of the particular aspects of their life will be highlighted here. The chapter is prepared only from written documents available and no field study is made to any extent.

The Boros or the Boro Kacharis form a very important part in the population of Assam. They belong to the Indo-Mongoloid racial stock. The Boro group includes several tribes some of which are Kachari, Rabha, and Hajong etc. The Kacharis of lower Assam are referred to as Boro Kachari. Chatterjee (1974) writes about Boros, "The Bodos, who spread over the whole of the Brahmaputra valley and North Bengal as well as East Bengal forming a solid block in North Eastern India, and they form one of the main basis of the present day population of these tracts".

Because of the co-existence with the people of the country, the Boros are acculturated, but they retain their tribal group identity. There is also the assimilation and fusion in case of their folklore materials, but they retain their own distinctness. So naturally, the folk literatures of the Boros have similarity to those of the other tribes and people of Assam. On the other hand, the Boros have the settlements in the entire Brahmaputra valley, and as a result of which they have a remarkable contribution towards the growth and development of the Assamese culture.

The Boros have folk songs connected with seasonal and agricultural festivals and ceremonies. These festivals are known as *Baisagu Methay* and *Domachi Methay*. The marriage song is known as *Haba Methay*. They have also their ethnic term to suggest the songs associated with rites and rituals. *Kherai* songs are chanted during *Kherai* worship.

Patriotism, the edification of the dignity of labour, the consequence of any indiscreet action, tolerance, patience in the time of dilemma are the main trend of knowledge that are revealed in the folk songs of the Boros. Another remarkable trend of knowledge is their philosophical and spiritual ideas. In many of the songs of the Boros, cosmogonic ideas like eternity, time or space etc., are revealed clearly.

In one of the songs, the advice is given not to loose heart in disaster and misery. The duty of a man is to face bravely the misfortune and calamities that may come to one's life. The mystery of the world is enigmatic and cannot be understood easily:

"In times of distress, and misery,
One should have fortitude,
Not one can fathom the mysteries of creation
Of the Lord of our world" (Brahma, 1960)

The Boros believe that behind every action there is God. They believe in oneness of the human soul and the natural world. Transistorises of the created things are expressed in the following refrain:

'Trees and creepers and shrubs
And the elephants and the horses
All are created by Him
Listen, Oh: You man;
None of them lasts forever' (Brahma, 1960)

The Boros are hard working people. Origina'ly, they engaged in shifting cultivation. Bullocks are necessary for their agricultural life. Therefore, in a song there is a sugg stion to drive the cattle safely towards home before the settii. ; of the sun. It is noteworthy that in the Rig Veda also there are a few hymns where safety and well-being of the cattle is sung. The shed door should also be closed carefully otherwise, the cow may be victims of tigers that are roaming around. For *Jhum* cultivation, they clear the land by setting fire in the forest. They invite Baobuli, the god of the wind to help them spreading fire in the forest.

The quality of various things necessary in their day-to-day life is also expressed in their songs. For example, a good quality of loom can be made from *Sal* tree. Therefore, the wife asks her husband for a loom and a shuttle made up of *Sal* wood:

'Fetch me oh: Dear,
A shuttle made of Sal wood' (Brahma, 1960)

Besides the idea of imitating, the colourful objects of natural world can also be found in their songs. So the Boro girl dreams of weaving the butterfly in their woven cloths. In an agricultural society cornful of granary and shedful of cows, bear a great importance. These are even the criteria for marriage of a girl to a groom.

Another important kind of knowledge is revealed through the folk songs, which is used as a piece of advice to the newly wedded bridegrooms. Whether a bride does good or bad, but the bride belongs to the groom and any kind of loss sustained to the bride is the loss of the bridegroom. The bridegroom should consider the bride as his own life partner sharing her joys and sorrows. This attitude is very important in the present society also where women have to face ill treatment from her male counterpart.

'But be mindful of duties
If you break limbs,
The loss will be your own
For, she is your life's partner' (Brahma, 1960)

The simple folk are very much conscious of swift moving time, which is also the subject matter of many of the sophisticated literature of the world. Fleeing time cannot be regained. Once it is lost, it is lost forever. Such highly philosophical knowledge is revealed through a marriage song that is used to console a bride:

"Time, in eternal motion
Advanced bit by bit
Before we are aware,
Or before we are serious about our duties.
The past recedes, the future arrives
Do not remain fast asleep,
Losing your own self in delusion' (Brahma, 1960).

This is surprising that these unlettered people, only with the strength of their accumulated experience, seemed to be very much conscious of the idea of eternity and the cosmic order of the universe. They are least aware of the philosophical theories. However, these simple, rustic songs express more than thousand theories of philosophy. These couplets, here, warn man of their short span to be spent in this world. Life is very short in respect to the time infinite and if they are not conscious of their assigned duties, their soul surely will be enveloped by deluded potency of ignorance. Therefore, they must do their duties within the allotted time because time passes unnoticed. This is an excellent specimen of higher wisdom expressed in abject simplicity of ideas.

The Boros hate gluttony and slothness. Their folk songs warn not to eat too much like a pig. These songs even express fright saying to men that God will send tigers to punish the gluttons. The need of defending their country was felt by the Boros. They awake the sense of patriotism to the minds of the young people. Probably the inhabitants of Bhutan were the threat to the sovereignty of their country. Therefore, through their songs they teach their people to love their motherland and to protect her from the impending danger that may come from intruders. The following song tries to infuse courage and heroism in the mind of their people. They must wield shield and sword for defense of their motherland:

'We are the sons of heroes,
We know not fear,
The shield and the sword,
Are our playthings – our boys' (Brahma, 1960)

Their love for the motherland is so great that they even think of cutting the enemy into pieces. When the enemies are, marching ahead the legendary hero should tighten the reins and use the spur to make the horse run fast. When the motherland is in danger, no distinction should be made between man and woman.

Apart from these songs laden with knowledge saying, the Boros have their adages full of knowledge. These sayings are of immense practical values, as these evolved from true experiences of eventful life. It is the creation of the collective masses finding expression through the wit of one. Among the tribes of Africa, proverbs are used as law. "Proverbs tell us a lot, but a fact that is not sufficiently emphasised seemed to be that they show that the rural folk have a definite outlook on life's problem or that they may even constitute an ethics of living. Proverbs have a lot to say on, for instance, fair play, truthfulness, value of hard work, poverty etc"(Goswami, 1983).

Lack of proper judgment in doing a work or any decision taken quickly may lead to disaster. Besides unnecessary comments or loose talk may also cause danger:

'Man dies because of mouth' (Boro, 2001)
'That river which has strong currents soon acquires sand back' (Boro, 2001).

Such sayings are really the product of man's experience and these prove to be extremely true. The Boros have some proverbs regarding the health of a baby. If a baby has a loose motion, it should not be considered as a serious matter. Instead, it is a sign of the various changes that may take place in his growth. However, in case of a grown up man it should be taken seriously:

'The baby has a loose motion,
Only to grow up,
The old man has a loose motion only to die' (Boro, 2001)

The misdeeds of the children may cause great harm to the old. The parents have to pay dearly for their children's mischief. Therefore, the children should be given proper instruction. This particular aspect of knowledge is expressed in another proverb:

'You commit some crime and have litigation,
Your parents will have to bear the brunt of it' (Boro, 2001)

The advantage of buying a cow from neighbourhood is given stress in another proverb because such cow brought from a known locality can be found out easily if lost. On the other hand, in marrying a girl, one should go to far off places:

'See your bride in a far off place,
Buy the cow from your neighbourhood' (Boro, 2001).

One should give extreme attention in doing a particular work. Otherwise, the result may not be good enough. He should be alert from all sides keeping his sense organs ready:

> *'With the five sense organs of hearing*
> *Smell, sight, taste,*
> *With the five organs of work and sex*
> *Oh, Brother, with the black hair on your head,*
> *Jump into the river of life.'* (Boro, 2001).

These proverbs are created out of experience of the people and they reflect the mentality and the ways of life of the tribe. However, to understand the underlying meaning of these proverbs the context is important apart from the text. "The context of an item of folklore is the specific social situation where that particular item is employed" (Dundes, 1978). Malinowski also emphasised the importance of context saying, "without the context it becomes lifeless" (Malinowski, 1926).

Tales and myths are the embodiment of all kinds of folklore. So the tales of a particular community say much about the community including their manner of life, their faith, rites and rituals, the cause of the origin of things, the mystery behind a particular phenomenon, etc. At the time when there were no books, the imparting of education and knowledge was made through the myths and the tales. They can also be used as a pedagogic device using the moral of the story, which is always not so overt. They can give economic, social and political knowledge. It is worth mentioning that the *Panchatantra* was written to give the Princes of knowledge of politics, economics and social ethics. They work as a practical guide to the people. So Malinowski (1926) says about the function of a myth; "Myth serve as warrant, a charter and often even a practical guide".

The tales of the Boro Kachari also give some knowledge like the causes of separation among the brothers, origin of things or the idea that one should give too much weight upon the report given by others. In the tale *'Bhaye Bhaye Lage Kiya'* the seed of enmity was sown between brothers paying importance on wife's unnecessary complaints. Though it is warned against the wife, it is true in case of other people also. Before believing some body, one must consider the matter rationally.

For the smooth running of the family the cooperation and unity between husband and wife is necessary. Marriage is a matter of mutual adjustment. The tale of *Kathiya Budang, Chandramali* teaches the people to live together happily thinking that they are destine to be so. In another tale, *Tirotar Budhi Suniba Nalage,* a very important message is given and it is relevant even to day. When the wife was asked regarding the boon that her husband should ask, she had told not to ask the boon of becoming a king or a minister, as the common people dislike them. Besides, the normal life is disturbed very much. Another idea that is expressed through the tale is that no one should follow others blindly as blind support may bring disaster to man.

Many tales teach us not to take any decision in haste. Besides, one must be conscious of every thing keeping a watchful eye on every side. This idea is well expressed through tale like *Rajputrar Kahini* where a woman killed her faithful dog that was guarding her baby. She concluded that the dog killed her baby as she saw blood in the mouth of the dog. She killed her dog and had to repent for her indiscriminate deed.

In these tribal tales we find a very scientific method of proving the things whether they are edible or not. Whenever they had to eat anything for the first time, they used to feed it to the animals or birds like physician in having his test of medicines on rats or other animals today.

The sexual relationship among the incest was prohibited and the idea of it can be found in many tales. In the tale *Alari Dambra* (Sarma, 1997) the brother came to marry his sister Ashagi and Baisagir, who refused to do so. It is noteworthy that the modern medical science also does not prescribe relationship between incest. Besides, these people though were unlettered was keen observer of the natural phenomena. They attribute the origin of thunder and lightening to their mythical story. The Boros believe that these sisters mentioned above turned into lightening and Baubali (the brother) into thunder. So thunder is always accompanied by lightening.

The psychologists nowadays are always of the soothing effect of music by which many diseases can be cured. Every creature has an inherent love for music. A baby seemed to lull in sleep listening to music. In the pastoral life, the tribes used to play *Seraja* in tending their cattle that were enchanted by the music and usually did not go astray. This makes it easy for the cowboy to drive his cattle safely at home.

These are some of the traditional knowledge, which find expression through the folk literature of the Boros. Outwardly, these may look simple, but every bit of knowledge is saturated with true experience of their life and occupation. These were considered as worthy guidance to be followed by younger people in their rough and hard ways of life. These are taken as untold law and principle for the smooth running of the society. Degh (1972) makes an important remark about legends, which is worth mentioning – "The reason for telling a legend is basically not to entertain but to educate people, to inform them about an important fact, to warn them against danger within cultural environment. What Degh speaks of legend is also true in case of tales and myths of all the societies and of all the places.

References

Boro, A., 2001, *Folk Literature of the Bodos.* Guwahati: Adhunik Prakashan.

Bhahma, M.M., 1960, *Folksongs of the Bodos.* Guwahati: Publication Department, Gauhati University.

Chatterjee, S.K., 1974, *Kirata Janakriti.* Calcutta : Asiatic Society of Bengal.

Dandes, A. 1978, *Journal of Indian Folkloristic*, Vol 1.

Degh, L., 1972, "Legend Genres", in E.M. Dorson (Ed). *Folklore and Folk Life: An*

Introduction. Chicago: Chicago University Press

Goswami, P.D., 1983, *Essays on the Folklore and Culture of North Eastern India.* Guwahati : Spectrum Publication.

Malinowski, B., 1926, *Myths in Primitive Psychology.* London : Routledge and Kegan Paul Ltd.

Sarma, S., 1997, *Asamar Sadhukatha.* Guwahati : Bookhive.

Thompson, S., 1946, *The Folktale.* New York.

16

Jirkedam – A Traditional Institution Among the Karbis

Girin Das

The Karbis constitute the largest ethnic group among the hill tribes of Assam. They live predominantly in the autonomous hill district of Karbi Anglong. The district with a total geographical area of 10,434 sq.km. is also the largest district in the State. According to 2001 Census (Provisional), the total population in the district is 8.12 lakh out of which the Karbi population is 2.96 lakh. Besides the Karbis, other tribal communities such as the Dimasa Kacharis, Rengma Nagas, Garos, Khasis, Jaintias, Man-Tais and Kukis, etc., have been inhabiting the district since remote past. Moreover, there are settlements of Assamese, Bengalis, Tea and Ex-Tea Garden communities and Hindi speaking people in the district. Ethnically the Karbis are of Mongoloid origin. They belong to the Kuki-Chin group of the Tibeto-Burman sub-family of the Sino-Tibetan linguistic family. In this chapter, an attempt is being made to highlight the functions of one of their traditional institutions, the bachelors' dormitory *Jirkedam*.

Jirkedam

In ancient time, the Karbis were a nomadic tribe. They moved from place to place in search of *Jhum* land for their livelihood. As a result, they had no idea of establishing a village or any kind of social organisation. According to legends, with the incarnation of a great social reformer named Kachen, radical changes took place among them. Kachen was popularly known as Ru-Kachen, Ru meaning grandfather. He took the leadership of the Karbi community and initiated a settled social life by establishing the village Miring Rongchopi with one thousand families at Nongkula by the side of the river Kopili. The village headman *(Sarthe)* was Rangmukrang. Later on, Ru-Kachen suggested Harbaman, an able administrator, social activist and artist of repute to establish a village comprising one thousand families. Accordingly, he started a big village named Teron Rongchopo and decided to improve agriculture for the benefit of the people. For this purpose, he called a meeting of the village people and expressed his willingness to carry out co-operation of bachelors' dormitory *Jirkedam* that was the training center of non-formal education. It provided the opportunity of imparting education to the youths practically in relation to all aspects of their life viz., agricultural activities, socio-religious customs and practices, village administration and traditional art and crafts, etc. In fact, the Karbi culture started to blossom through the institution of *Jirekedam* which introduced festivals like *Ritnong Chindi, Henup Ahi Kekan* and *Hacha Kekan,* etc. It may be relevant to point out here that the institution of bachelors' dormitory is known by various terms like *Jirkedam, Maro, Terang Ahem, Terang Hangbar, Farla* and *Terang*, etc. The reasons for different terms may be due to varied geographical locations of the people in the district. However, the most popular term is *Jirkedam.*

The dormitory is a thatched pile-dwelling house, the interior portion of which is decorated with artistic design. It is built by the youths preferably in the middle of the village. All the unmarried boys of the village from 12 years of age are its members. They sleep at night in the dormitory. On the eve of *Rongker* festival, the boys approach the village headman for selecting the leader in order to carry out their activities for three years. The total number of office-bearers for smooth management of the institution is 26. The list of functionaries is as follows:

Klengsarpo - Leader

Klengdun - Assistant leader

Sodar kethe - Supervisor

Sodar so - Assistant supervisor

Barlon kethe / Tharlon po - Surveyor

Barlon so / Tharlon so	- Assistant surveyor
Motan ar-e	- Guide
Motan arvi	- Assistant Guide
Than ar-e	- Convener
Than arvi	- Assistant convener
Chengbrup kethe	- Chief drummer
Chengbrup so	- Assistant drummer
Me Apai	- Fire keeper
Lang Apai	- Water keeper
Kove thok	- Collector of betel nut
Bithi Thok	- Collector of betel leaf
Phankri kethe	- Distributor of betel nut
Phankri so	- Assistant distributor of betel nut
Arphek kethe	- Dormitory cleaner
Arphek so	- Assistant dormitory cleaner
Chinhak kethe	- Carrier of the basket of tools
Chinhak so	- Assistant carrier of the basket of tools
Sanghorai kethe	- In charge of maintenance of discipline in the Dormitory
Sanghorai so	- Assistant. in charge of maintenance of discipline in the Dormitory
Langbong kethe	- Water supplier
Langbong so	- Assistant water supplier

So far as associate membership of the girls in the dormitory is concerned, Medhi (1993) mentions, "A girl selected as an associate member is attached to one regular boy member by the leader *Klengsarpo* in consultation with *Risobasapi*, the wife of the junior village headman. *Risobasapi* talks freely with the girls in the matter and takes their opinion in selecting their partners. The mental make up of a girl, she likes, dislikes, age, and clan, etc., are taken into consideration in this matter.

The boy selected for a girl to be attached with, must not belong to the same clan. The boy's consent is also counted and in almost all cases, the relationship thus established is on mutual consent. In case of maladjustment between a girl and a boy, the pair is allowed to break and the leader makes a change. A girl selected as associate member is known as *Marpi*. This title *Marpi* is added after the designation of a boy member. The leader of the girl is attached to the leader of the boy, the *Klengsarpo* and she is known as the *Klengsarpo-a-Marpi*. She is selected on her personal qualifications like hard work, good physique, commanding ability and proficiency in dance and music. She must be willing to accept the responsibility besides accepting the *Klengsarpo* as an all time companion. Her duty is to control the girl members in the institution and to help the *Klengsarpo* in the maintenance of discipline among the girls". In this manner, other associate members are selected out of the adolescent girls of the village.

The literal meaning of *Jirkedam* is collective work or collective march. The young boys and girls proceed to the *jhum* fields from the dormitory under strict supervision, carry out their activities systematically and come back in the evening maintaining proper discipline. With regard to the functioning of *Jirkedam* in agricultural activities, Gohain (1984) narrates, "In the olden days any villager might approach the *Klengsarpo* and *Klengdun* offering them gourds of liquor for helping him in the field. *Klengsarpo* might accept the gourd and then would order the boys and the girls for collective work (*Jirkedam*) in the field of the villager. The boys and the girls would collect in front of the *Terang* and the *Tharlon po* would stand first with his measuring bamboo pole followed by the Assistant Drummer (*Chengbrup so*) on the left and the Chief Drummer on the right, followed by *Chinhak kethe, Chinhak so, Motan ar-e, Motan arvi* and others. The last boy would be the *Klengsarpo*. Then *Banwakpi* (cloth supplier) and *Banwak so* (assistant cloth supplier) amongst girls would follow. Other girls would follow these two. Foodstuff would be collected from house to house by *Phankri kethe* and *Phankri so*. The rice was given in packet of leaves and if there were any uneatable thing in the packet, the family would have to pay fine as punishment. The entrusted functionaries would carry these. In the field *Motan arvi* and

Motan ar-e would take right and left positions and *Barlon po* (*Tharlon po*) would measure the land. The entire plot would be divided into two parts. In one part, *Klengdun* would be in charge, in the other *Klengsarpo*. The *Putchekpo* would fix the index signs on the field and the *Klengdun* would take left side while *Klengsarpo* would take right side. All the functionaries with '*so*' suffix would take left side. The *Pyhankri kethe* and *Phankri so* would distribute betel nut. The other functionaries would supply specified items. After work, they would return to *Terang* systematically".

It may not be out of place to mention here that the Karbis practice *Jhuming (Inglong Arit)* through various stages of operation. These are:

Ritkepan - The felling of trees and clearing of the undergrowths in February (*Thang Thang*)

Mekekai - The burning of the debris in April (*Jangmi*)

Arhikkarhi - The removal of half-burnt logs in May (*Aru*) and June (*Vosik*)

Rik - Sowing of various types of seeds as soon as rains start

Sok karlu - Weeding of plants in July (*Jakhong*)

Sok kerot - Harvesting of *Ahu* paddy in August (*Pai pai*) and *Sali* paddy in October (*Phre*)

Thus, it is seen that the young boys and girls of the dormitory get the scope of acquiring sufficient knowledge of *jhum* operations and prevailing weather conditions. Moreover, they learn about edible fruits, roots, tubers, leaves and medicinal plants and herbs, etc., available in the forests.

In addition to agricultural activities, the boys carry out wooden, bamboo and cane works in the dormitory while the girls spin *endi* and cotton yarns and weave clothes with varieties of floral and faunal designs in their traditional loin looms (*Therang*). It may be mentioned here that the Karbi boys are expert in making wooden articles such as spoons for distributing boiled rice, saucepan for keeping boiled rice, stool, mortar, pestle and bamboo and cane articles such as sieve, winnowing tray, various types of baskets, fishing implements, loin loom, fan and sleeping mat, etc. Similarly, the girls weave traditional dresses like *Pini* (*mekhela*), *Wamkok* (piece of cloth worn like a belt), *Jiso* (piece of cloth taken over breasts), *Rikong* (loincloth), *Choi* (shirt), *Poho* (hat), *endi chadars* and other necessary clothes for their day-to-day use. The presence of *Jirkedam* boys and girls in any festival particularly in marriage ceremony, *Chomangkan* (death ceremony) is highly essential since they have to perform assigned duties under the leadership of *Klengsarpo*. Moreover, they extend helping hand towards the poor, widows and destitute of the village. It is interesting to note that dance and music form an integral part of Karbi life and culture. Therefore, the adult members of the dormitory come forward to teach the juniors about traditional dance and music. The juniors also learn folk tales, folk songs and ballads, etc., from the senior ones. Moreover, *Ubebarium* (adviser of the bachelors' dormitory), an aged and wise person imparts training on the art of handicrafts and about the Karbi culture. Thus, it is observed that *Jirkedam* not only enhances the spirit of co-operation, sense of discipline and eagerness of social service among the youths but also offers the young boys and girls the opportunity to acquire knowledge in respect of their rich cultural heritage. However, such a vital institution could not withstand the onslaught of time and became outdated. Perhaps the primary factors for such a situation are the spread of modern education, development activities, introduction of settled cultivation, influence of Christianity and acculturation, etc.

Although *Jirkedam* is not to be found among the Karbis in its original form, its existence is seen in the interior areas of Karbi Anglong district in a rudimentary form. Based on a study, Das (1993) mentions, "However, we find reminiscence of the dormitory institution in the remote areas of this district. For example, in Patikindok village, about 13 km from Ulukunchi, the members of *Jirkedam* completed the period of 3 years in February 1991. Of course, the members did not sleep in the dormitory but they used to sleep at night in their own homes. In Wanpung village under Baithalangso Police Station, *Jirkedam* is performed for 4-5 months i.e., during cultivation period only. In Dokhara Bey Village under Bokajan Police Station, the youths use a part of the residence of the village headman for their meetings and other occasions. It may, therefore, be assumed that the future Karbi generations would be quite at dark about the manifold activities of this institution unless the District Council authority comes forward to undertake certain positive measures for revival of the dormitory in some form or other, considering its glorious past, in toto".

Concluding Observations

Jirkedam played a vital role in educating the Karbi youths in traditional set-up. The boys and girls could learn all aspects of their socio-cultural, political and religious life. Thus, the knowledge they acquired through the dormitory institution inspired them to lead their future life safely in specific geo-environmental settings. However, things have now changed. Revival of this institution in its traditional form will not be accepted by the youths. While dealing with the *Nokpante* (dormitory) system of the Garos, Majumdar (1984) comments, "The structure of the Garo society in which the institution of dormitory thrived is no longer there, so, the dormitory in its original form has lost the right of existence. The author as a Block Development Officer in an interior area in Garo Hills once ardently tried to revive the dormitory in its original form in non-Christian traditional villages. Money was given for the construction of grand buildings of the original type. Musical instruments of all sorts (including harmonium and gramophones) were given to attract the bachelors to sleep in the dormitories. However, all these could no more attract the boys to sleep in the dormitories and gradually these buildings decayed, or the villagers themselves dismantled these buildings and used the posts and beams for their own dwelling house. Apparently the institution has lost its moorings, and probably it will never come to life in its original form". Similarly, regarding the institution *Zawlbuk*, Chakravarty (1989) opines, "The decline of the institution *Zawlbuk* (although N.E. Parry tried his utmost to keep it alive in the Lushai Hills District by an executive order) is a study in melancholy, because contact with urban agencies and the winds of change proved disastrous for the institution. In fact, there is now no *Zawlbuk* in the entire Jampui and Sakhan Hills".

It is; therefore, felt that instead of reviving *Jirkedam* in its original form, efforts may be made for forming an institution on identical ideology with the initiative of the present-day youths. This institution will act as the nucleus for promoting traditional dance and music, games and sports, art and crafts, etc. Moreover, the dormitory spirit will inspire them to render social service to the community, undertake co-operative farming with modern agricultural methods and serve as the vital force in political matters. Over and above, the future life of the youths will be deeply rooted to their traditional culture. Ultimately, the Karbi youths will march ahead for a better tomorrow in a cohesive and integrated manner, thus, bringing an end to the ongoing fratricidal clashes among them and restoring peace and tranquility in the society.

References

Chakravarty, M., 1989, "Continuity and Change: A Case Study in Tripura", in J.B. Bhattacherjee (Ed): *Sequences of Development in North East India*. pp. 215-222, New Delhi: Omsons Publications.

Das, G. N., 1993, *Traditional Tribal Institutions of the Hill Areas of Assam*. Diphu : District Research Office.

Gohain, B., 1984, *The Hill Karbis*. Diphu: Smt. Arunima Gohain.

Majumdar, D.N., 1984, "A decaying institution - What has happened to the Nokpante? : A study among the Garos ", in S. Karotemprel and B. Dutta Roy (Ed.) : *The Tribes of North East India*. pp. 307-318. Calcutta: Firma KLM Private Limited.

Medhi, G.C., 1993, "Women: Their Training and Status in Karbi Society", in B.C. Bhuyan (Ed): *The Tribal Women*. pp. 32-38. New Delhi: Omsons Publication.

17

Megalithic Tradition– The Case of the Karbis in North East India

Dwipen Bezbaruah

The term megalith in archaeology has a wide connotation. It is defined as a tomb built with prodigious rude stone or pit dug in soft rock where remains of the dead human are deposited and stones erected for commemorative or funerary purpose. Besides graves without any lithic assemblages but by virtue of possessing, certain other materials like pottery are also classified as megaliths. To quote Gordon Childe (1947), "The term megalith is derived from Greek words (*mega* = large and *lithos* = stones) and is originally introduced by antiquaries to describe a fairly definable class of monuments in western and northern Europe consisting of huge undressed stones and termed in Celtic as dolmen, cromlech and menhir". Daniel wrote, "It might be thought logical to apply the term 'megalithic' to all constructions using very large roughly dressed slabs of stones....... but in archaeology, it is customary to restrict the term megalithic monuments to certain specific types of constructions employing these large stones – chamber tombs, rows, single standing stone, enclosures, which were in the main constructed between 2000 BC and 1500 BC". Megalithic structures consist of single piece of erected stone termed menhir or complex passage graves with box shaped stone grave at one end with entrance made of stone. Rac (1996), however, classifies the megaliths into two broad categories – the sepulchral monuments that are burial proper and the non-sepulchral ones, which are commemorative in nature. Besides the ideational and socio-cultural meanings and practices with megaliths are many and vary with communities. The universal occurrence of megaliths is a matter that evokes serious thoughts. Its occurrence is reported from European territories, South and Southeast Asia, Mediterranean region, Africa, Near Eastern territories, Polynesian and Melanesian islands etc. In India, occurrence of megaliths is reported from South Indian States of Karnataka, Andhra Pradesh, Tamil Nadu and Maharashtra, the Chotanagpur and Bastar regions of Central and Eastern India, North and Northeastern States. Sepulchral varieties occur more frequently in South India comprising many structures as pit burials, urn burials. The South Indian megalithic culture is associated with Iron Age weapons and pottery (mainly black and red ware) recovered through systematic explorations and excavation and dated back to the first millennium B.C. in the Iron Age. In Central and Northeastern India the commemorative ones such as menhir (single piece of upright stone), dolmen (stone slab placed horizontally on three or more smaller pieces of stone) occur and the practice is still prevalent as a living tradition among certain tribal communities.

The Living Megalithic Practice

As mentioned earlier, megalithic practice has survived as a living practice among some tribal communities in Eastern, Central and North Eastern India. Furer-Haimendorf (1945) reports that the Bastar Gond, Hill Marias, Dorlas and Murias erect menhirs (*uraskal*) and sometimes dolmens (*danyakal*) as memorial to the dead and the erection is generally accompanied by feast and the sacrifice of a cow and a bullock. Among the Mundas of Chotanagpur, large stone slab cover certain graves and dolmen supported by smaller stones serving as family burial place where bones of the family members are buried. Other Munda speaking tribes and Hos also have identical megalithic practice. The Gadabas, Bondus and Keenghar of Orissa have the tradition of erecting menhirs, dolmens and stone circles for commemorative and funerary purposes. Stone erection with a feast of merit is reported among the Gadabas. Similarly, Keenghar erect menhirs when the head of the village dies. Besides stones, some tribes also erect wooden posts. Thus, the Koyas of Hyderabad erect a temporary forked post on the place where the memorial feast is performed and sacrificed cows are invariably tied to these posts. Square wooden post are also erected by the Korkus of Central West India and Raj Gonds of Hyderabad in course of the memorial feast of the dead individual. Large stone slabs locally known as *sasandri* cover certain graves like the dolmen supported by smaller stones serves as family burial place where parts of the bones of the family members are buried in the course of a second funeral; menhirs locally known as *bidri* are set alongside the *sasandri* the grave or.in other places along the village roads.

North East India occupies a prominent place in the archaeological map of the world because of the rich megalithic remains. It is one of the few places in the world, where this practice has survived as a living practice. Realising the significance of North East Indian megaliths, Mills (1933) reports, "An ethno archaeological characteristic of Assam of worldwide fame is its wealth of megaliths. Indeed it is one of the few places in the world where monuments of this type are still erected." Although none of the megalithic structures of the North East India has yet been dated, it is agreed by all scholars that the custom of erection prevailed in North East India from prehistoric period (Clarke, 1847). In North East India, megaliths are spread over a wide territory across the States of Arunachal Pradesh, Nagaland, Manipur, Mizoram; North Cachar hills, Karbi Anglong, Nagaon, Morigaon and Kamrup districts of Assam and eastern part of Meghalaya. Sharma (1984) comments that the greatest concentration of megaliths in North East India is observed in the Khasi and Jayantia hills districts of Meghalaya and that the region houses some of the largest piece of menhirs.

The Living Megalithic Practice among the Karbis

Erection of stone in the form a menhir with a table stone in front is still prevalent among the Karbis living in the plains areas of undivided Kamrup, Nagaon and Morigaon districts of Assam as a post-cremation rite. Compared to their hill counterparts, the plain Karbis mainly inhabiting parts of Southern Kamrup, Nagaon and Morigaon districts of Assam have been acculturated and many elements of Assamese caste Hindu society have penetrated into their life ways. However, stone erection as post-cremation rite has still survived among them as a living example of a primitive tradition. Among the plain Karbis, elaborate rites and rituals can be observed during the erection of the stone structures. Phangso (2000) also mentions about the existence of the stone erection practice among the Karbis for commemorating the dead. He, however, has not recorded the details of the practice.

The erection of the stone is carried out generally within one month of the death of a person as a post-cremation rite. The family of the deceased and the entire village participate in the ceremony. The village headman and the *Kathar,* the religious head, play an important role in the performance of the ceremony. The village headman in consultation with the family members, delegates various responsibilities to different members of the village for successfully holding the ceremony.

As the first step of the ceremony, villagers bring the stone from nearby mountain. Generally, four young persons including one from the house of the dead along with the priest are sent to bring the stone. The group of people carry with them certain items such as one gourd filled with rice beer (locally known as *Horlang*) which is a must item for all socio-religious functions besides betel leaves and areca-nuts, one pot of the basil water (*tulsi pani*) and rice flour. The dry gourd shell is carried to predict the fate of the dead by breaking the gourd shell on the stone. If the broken shell of the gourd falls in the same position, it indicates that the person has died at the right time and age and if the broken parts fall in the opposite direction, the person is believed to have died premature. The other items are carried to appease and propitiate the stone. The stone is then worshipped with chanting of hymns. The stones, preferably one round and the other triangular are then cleaned, washed with water and purified with rice beer and then tied with coir rope and carried to the megalithic field. In some villages, a bier is made to carry the stones in the same manner as the corpse is carried in the bier to the cremation ground.

The stones are finally erected in the megalithic field. The triangular stone is erected vertically and the round stone is placed horizontally supported by four slabs of stone underneath. The vertically erected stone called *Long-e* that signifies the dead while the horizontally placed piece of stone called *Long-dang* (also called *sangei* in some places) serves as a plate on which food is offered to the dead. However, no material goods are offered to the dead. In case of male, a white piece of cloth is tied on the top of the stone in the form of a turban called locally as *Ponho* while in case of a female the cloth is wrapped in the form of *Mekhela* (cloth worn by the Assamese female) and a red thread is tied at the top.

Erection of stone accompanied animal sacrifice in Karbi society. Sacrifice of fowl is made in every rites and ritual. Fowls besides pig are sacrificed on the place of erection of megaliths. The family of the deceased should offer the first stock of animals on the *Long-dang*. Rice beer is also offered in a bamboo tube and is placed on the right side of the *Long-dang*. Sometimes, two branches of coral trees (*madar*) are also planted besides the *Long-dang*. The ceremony ends with the *Kathar* invoking the spirit of the dead to rest on the main pillar of the house of the dead person's family through chanting of hymns.

In case of death of a person with poor family background, the dead body is carried to the cremation ground in a simple bamboo bier tied with a coir rope. Cremation is not followed by stone erection for such person considering the elaborateness and expenses involved. However, for others, the dead body is carried to the cremation ground in a bamboo bier made of two pieces of bamboo placed in a parallel position and smaller pieces placed across them. However, this does not indicate the difference in post-cremation ritual with the difference in economic status, as such, and man of average economy performs stone erection. However, the ethnographic account of Lyall (1908) points to the existence of the stone erection ceremony in the case of a person with high social status in Karbi society. Lyall recorded the custom as follows:

"If a great man, such as a *mauzadar* or leading *gaonbura* (*sardar, sarthe*), dies, in addition to the ceremony (usual)......., there is another, called *Langtuk* (the well). A well or pit is dug outside the village, four-square, with sides ten to fifteen feet;

it need not be carried down to the water; stairs are made to the bottom. At the corners are planted various trees. A tall upright (*long-chang*) and a broad flat stone (*long-pak*) supported on short uprights, are brought and set up, as in the Khasi Hills. The *risomar* comes and dances there the whole day with manifold apparatus. The *Uchepi* sings and places food of different kind on the flat stones, with flowers. A fowl is killed for the well at the bottom of the pit, and their heads thrown to the *risomar*. Then the people of thirty to forty villages assemble. The *Uchepi* extemporaneously dances before the memorial stone, and the people dance and eat there until dark...........The *Langtuk* is very costly, for people have to be fed at two places, and double the quantity of food for an ordinary funeral has to be provided".

Megalithic Practices in North East and Central India

The tribal societies of North East India are reported to have elaborate practices of megalithic erection. The megalithic tradition of North East India were recorded and discussed at different periods by various scholars. The writings of the scholars threw light on various aspects of megalithic tradition from structural variations to socio-ideological beliefs and practices associated with it.

The Khasis and the Nagas are the notable tribes of North East India known to be associated with megalithic erection. Various sections of the Naga tribes like the Ao, Angami, Sema, Maram, Rengma, Konyak and others are known to have this practice amongst them. The western Angamis erect menhirs both as monument to the dead and as memorials of social accomplishments of the living. Rich men put up menhirs in the course of great feast of merit by which they gain social prestige and rank. Even when a menhir is erected in the honour of the dead man, a feast of merit must be held by his son in the name of the deceased person erection is solely to enhance the prestige of the living. Besides menhirs, stone sitting places sometimes consisting of several ascending rows of seats along with tanks or streams in certain cases are erected by the Nagas to contain the grave of clan ancestors. Shadap Sen (1981) writes that even among the Nagas, whose megaliths do not seem very closely linked with the cult of the dead, thought of the afterlife is not completely absent. The ceremonial feast of the Angami is of seven grades, according to their cost, size and duration. Erection of only wooden monuments commemorates feast of the sixth grade. On the other hand, monoliths erected as memorials have those of the seventh grade. Heine (1928) commented that according to the Angamis a man dies seven times, each time falling to a deeper underworld and he apparently thinks that these feasts are linked with this belief. Possibly one purpose of the feasts of merit, even if implicit only, is to help the soul of the donor in his successive afterlife.

The Karbis are neighbours of the Khasi who are already recognised as a megalithic community. The Khasi menhirs are erected in a linear pattern that generally consists of uneven number of stones. The tallest of the stones is generally placed at the middle and is occasionally ornamented with a small stone. These groups of Khasi megaliths may probably represent clan burial. In the front of the line of the menhirs, a large flat table stone resting on stone support is placed. The largest table stone are to be seen at Nartiang in the Jayantia hills and Lailongkoti in the Khasi hills of North East India. Sometimes two table stones are found parallel to one another. The table stones are always placed towards the middle of the group generally in front of the great central menhir. These groups of stones are usually situated alongside roads or close to well-known lanes / routes where they readily attract the attention of passers by. Gurdon (1914) classifies the megaliths of the Khasis into three groups:

1. Menhirs or Vertical Stones
2. Table Stones or Dolmen
3. Stone Cromlechs or Cairn.

Rao (1993) opines that second group of stones are strictly speaking not dolmen as they are not graves but are simply memorials. Thus, Rao classifies the megaliths of Khasi hills into two broad groups (i) Funerary Stones and (ii) Memorial Stones. The funerary stones are those stone tombs which was directly associated with the post-cremation ritual including the disposal of the remains of the deceased. Memorial stones include the menhirs and table stones that are put up by clansmen for the dead or to commemorate an event. The megalithic tradition of the Khasis, tells about a closely-knit matrilineal tradition. That a prominent position is given to the eldest maternal uncle is reflected in the stone monuments with a taller central memorial stone (*mawkni*) thus reflecting the matrilineal solidarity in the Khasi social organisation.

Stone circles are reported to serve as memorials for rich tribesmen among the Nagas. Hutton (1922) reports that the Marring villages of Nagaland have their sacred enclosures circles of stones with a stone in the middle. Shakespeare (1914) mentions records of Naga circle of thirty-two large stones in conjunction with a row of fourteen menhirs, within which ritual dances are held at an annual feast in commemoration of the dead. Circular enclosures usually made up of smaller stones known as *kpep* among the Khasis are reported as not such common type.

Compared to the Nagas and the Khasis, the structural significance of the Karbi megaliths is not that elaborate. The dominant megalithic structures of the Karbis are menhir and dolmenoid-menhir. The functional aspect of the menhir in the Karbi society is the representation of the deceased, which is similar largely to other tribes like the Nagas and the Khasis. As far as the ritual aspect is concerned, tribal communities have elaborate rites followed by animal sacrifice. Thus, in Karbi society dolmenoid-menhirs are put in honour of the dead, and the family of the deceased holds a feast in the name of the deceased member in which pig, fowls must be sacrificed, and the villagers are entertained with food and rice-beer. The custom is similar to that of the Nagas, but the Karbis do not erect menhirs as the Nagas do to augment the prestige and prosperity of the donor through feast of merit. Moreover, the prominent position given to the maternal uncle is not reflected through any stone monuments.

The Karbis in the past were also reported to have erected memorial stones (Lyall, 1908). Such stones are set up by the Karbis only in the memory of the important personage such as *mauzadars* or leading *gaonburahs*. Gurdon (1904) believes that the Karbi stones like the Khasi are mere cenotaphs, the ashes of the deceased Karbi being left at the burning places, which are generally by the side of the rivers and the memorial stones being necessarily anywhere near the burning grounds. As with the Khasi, feast and entertainments are given when the stone of the Karbis are erected but they need not necessarily consist of uneven numbers (Gurdon, 1904). Gurdon believes that it is possible that the Karbis have obtained the custom of erecting memorial stones from their neighbours, the Khasis.

The erection of these stone monuments among the Karbis is a living tradition as prevalent among the plain Karbis. The hill Karbis along with the plain Karbis practiced this tradition in the past as reported by Lyall (1908). The primitive megalithic monuments are very huge in size but the size of the recently erected structures is smaller in comparison to the former one. The Karbi stone monuments are found also with a flat stone in front of the erected one from the past to recent period. Furer-Haimendorf (1945) reports that most of the Bastar Gonds, Hill Marias, Bison-horn Marias, Dorlas and Murias erect menhirs locally known as *uraskal* and sometimes also dolmens known as *danyakal* as memorials to the dead. A feast and the sacrifice of a cow or bullock, which corresponds closely to the custom of the Gadabas, the Khasis and the Western Angami Nagas usually, accompany the erection. The idea that the dead honoured by memorial stone can render active help to their living kinsmen. The Mundas of Chotanagpur were reported to have erected menhirs known as *bidri* as memorials to the dead, and besides they had on the public meeting places, a sitting platform composed of large stone-slabs and such platforms are known as *sodors* among the Gadabas. Concerning the menhirs and dolmenoid-menhirs at Rongali in Karbi Anglong believed to have erected them to mark the public meeting place. Elwin (1955) reports the worshipping of wooden and stone pillars by the Marias, sacrifice buffalo and offer rice and worship these stones in the belief that the spirit of the dead reside in them. Worshipping of menhirs at Kamarpha by Karbis and contiguous Tiwas to propitiate the spirit of the ancestors who is believed to reside in them is a similar practice. The following table (Table 17.1) will clarify the differences and similarities in the megalithic practices of the Nagas, the Khasis, the Karbis and tribes of Central India:

Table 17.1. Comparison of Megalithic Practice

Tribes	*Nature of the Practice*	*Megalithic Structures Erected*
Nagas	Commemorative. Feast of Merit.	Menhir, dolmen, cist, stone-platform
Khasi	Funerary, Commemorative. Associated with bone-deposition	Menhir,dolmen,dolmenoid-menhir, stone enclosures, cist
Karbis	Commemorative. Associated with post-cremation rite	Menhir, dolmenoid-menhir.
Central India Tribes like Gond Murias, Dorlas, Mundas etc.	Commemorative. Sometimes associated with post-cremation rite.	Menhir, dolmen and stone-platform.

"Kuki-Chin, Karbi and even the Kachari culture and the megaliths of South-east Asiatic type can not be ignored". Such observations of various scholars and the present finding leads to the inference that the Karbis were the architects of the megaliths spread through North Cachar hills, hills of western Karbi Anglong and the plain region of Assam inhabited by the Karbis.

An analysis of the erection of megaliths as a post-cremation ritual prevalent among a section of the Karbis reveals many absorbing facts. First, it confirms the place of the Karbis among the megalithic communities of North East India, which Furer-Haimendorf (1945) terms as the Eastern India Megalithic Complex wherein he includes the tribes of Central India. It further indicates the presence of a more evolved form of worshipping the dead, which is well knit to their socio-cultural system. The ritualistic use of rice beer and sacrifice of birds and animals to commemorate and worship the ancestor has been doubtlessly a part of the religious system of the early farmers. Furer-Haimendorf (1945) comments thus,

"Ethnologically it is important that this megalithic culture of the South East Asiatic type, as we may conveniently call it, is mainly concentrated among tribes of well developed agricultural civilisations, characterised by the use of hoes, shifting cultivation on hill-fields and sometimes also permanent cultivation on irrigated terraces and the keeping of cattle for slaughter but not for use in the yoke or for milking. It is not found in the more primitive strata of Indian aboriginal cultures, neither the food gatherers nor hunters, such as the Chenchus and the jungle tribes of the Southwest, nor do the early digging-stick cultivators, such as Hill Baigas, show any trace of megalithic ritual". The Karbis who still practice megalithic erection have developed an agricultural system characterised by wet cultivation together with shifting cultivation. An examination of the hymns chanted by *Kathar,* the Karbi priest, on megalithic erection, reflects a deep concern over the well-being of the crops and cattle besides propitiating the soul of the dead. This indicates an underlying principle of fertility and generation behind megalithic erection among them and belief that their land and herd belonged to them because their forbearers had owned them. This conforms well to the observation made by Shadap Sen (1993), which states, " .....The spread of megalithic culture was associated with the cult of the ancestor (though not necessarily universal) as well as the principle of fertility and generation. Among the early farming communities the processes of birth and generation and those of fertility appeared to be so intimate that the two aspects of the same mystery found symbolic expressions in their customs and rituals".

Furer-Haimendorf (1945) hints the association of Neolithic culture with the spread of megalithic ritual in Asia and India in tune with Heine (1928) and other scholars. According to this view, people with Quadrangular Adze culture speaking early forms of Malayo-Polynesian languages are responsible for the spread of megalithic culture in Southeast Asia and Eastern India. These groups pushed through Indonesia and beyond taking with them the cult of megaliths. In their progress in mainland Southeast Asia, they met and mixed with men of another culture of mainland Southeast Asia known as Shouldered Axe culture associated with people speaking languages of Mon-Khmer type who learnt the use of megalith from people with Quadrangular Adze culture. Possibly some of them migrated to India taking their megalithic culture with them, and became one of the ancestors of the Munda speaking tribes of more recent time. This hypothesis presupposes a relationship between the Mon-Khmer and the Munda language. The Neolithic materials from Indonesia and Pacific suggests that there has been an amalgamation of these two industries which occurred probably in the Asiatic mainland and resulted in the polished Shouldered Adze with Quadrangular section as reported by Furer-Haimendorf (1945). Exploration in Karbi Anglong has resulted in the discovery of Polished Shouldered Adze with quadrangular section (Medhi *et al*, 1998) and this has further substantiated the observation made by Furer-Haimendorf who himself collected similar Neolithic tool type from the Naga Hills.

The survival and continuity of the megalithic practice among the Karbis can be examined in the light of the observation made by Rao (1977) in his scholarly discussion on the survival and continuity of Neolithic tradition in North East India. He thus commented "......In the case of North East India, where the environment exerts a profound influence on cultural development, resulting in the continuity and survival of cultures from the prehistoric past down to the present.........The nuclear area of Brahmaputra Valley with its fertile alluvial plains has fostered in its lap a civilisation characterised by relative complexity. The *cul de sac* or areas of isolation show a harmonious adjustment of physical and cultural environment, enabling the hill folk to subsist on *jhumming* or shifting cultivation supplemented by hunting and fishing. The hill people living in the areas of relative isolation are to some extent acculturated owing to their proximity to the Brahmaputra valley. It is in the area of isolation that we can trace this cultural continuity and survival". The Karbis of Assam have been living in isolation for years in an environment that reflects a harmonious adjustment of physical and cultural environment. The Karbis practice *jhum* besides wet cultivation and also hunting and fishing. Under such conditions, the continuity and survival of many primitive traditions is possible, including megalithic erection as a post-cremation rite.

The discontinuation of the practice among the hill Karbis in contrast to their counterpart in the plains of Assam has various explanations. The generally accepted view is the process of conversion to Christianity on a large scale. However, it fails to explain why this practice ceased among the non-Christian hill Karbis. Lyall (1908) observed that the original abode of the Karbis was the eastern most part of the Khasi-Jayantia territory bordering on the Kopili River. The folk tales of the Karbis also as stated by Bordoloi (1987) indicate that during reigns of the Kachari kings, the Karbis were driven to the hills and some of them entered into Jaintiapur, the erstwhile Jayantia kingdom and lived under the Jayantia suzerainty. As mentioned earlier, the megalithic tradition of Khasi-Jayantia territory is more elaborate and primitive in nature. Thus, it can be assumed that they borrowed the practice of megalithic erection from the Khasis during their early stage of farming marked by *jhumming*. This group possibly migrated to the plains and continued this practice in a more settled habitation facilitated by wet cultivation. Accepting the view of Phangso (1989) that the Karbis entered Assam in different waves of history, the later entrants to the hills were perhaps not accustomed to this practice but had magico-religious beliefs associated with the existing structures. Their conversion to Christianity in due course of time on a large scale alienated them from this tradition. This is further established by the absence of megalithic ruins in eastern part of Karbi Anglong similar to the types recorded in western part.

References

Bordoloi, B.N.; G.C. Sharma Thakur and M.C. Saikia, 1987, *Tribes of Assam,* pp. 52 – 71, Part – I, Guwahati: Tribal Research Institute, Assam.

Childe, V. Gordon, 1948, *Megaliths in Ancient India,* pp. 4-13, Part IV, New Delhi.

Clark, C. B., 1974, "The Stone Monuments of Khasi Hills". *Journal of Royal Anthropological India,* 3: 481 – 523.

Furer Haimendorf, C. Von., 1945, "The Problem of Megalithic Culture in Middle India", *Man in India,* 25, 2: 73 – 90.

Gurdon, P. R. T., 1907, *The Khasis,* London: David Nutt.

Heine, G., 1928, "Die Megalithen Sudostasiens and ihre Bedeuntrung". *Anthropos,* 23: 276 – 315.

Heine, G., 1958, Das Megalitheco problam. pp. 162=82, *Heritage Osterreichs zur Erforschung de Varganpenleit und Kulturegeschichte der Menchtriet Symposium.*

Hutton, J. H., 1922, "The Meaning and Method of Erection of Megaliths by the Naga Tribe". *Journal of Royal Anthropological Institute.* 52: 242-249.

Lyall, S.C., 1908, *The Mikir,* London : David Nutt.

Medhi, D.K., 1998, "On the Need of a Megalithic Monument Conservation Day". *Souvenir of Second Megalithic Monument Conservation Day.* Rangali, Hamren, Karbi Anglong, Assam.

Mills, J.P. and J.H.Hutton, 1929, "Ancient Monoliths of North Cachar".*Journal of Asiatic Society of Bengal.* 25: 285 – 300.

Phangso, P.C., 1988, *The Khasi – A Spatio-temporal Analysis in Tribal Economy.* Unpublished Ph.D Thesis, Gauhati University, Guwahati, Assam.

Phangso, P. C., 1999, *Karbi Anglong – Prakriti Aru Manuh.* Howrahghat, Karbi Anglong : Phukan Prakashan.

Rao, S.N., 1977, "Continuity and Survival of Neolithic Tradition in North Eastern India". *Asian Perspective.* 20, 2:

Rao, S.N., 1993, "Megalithic Practices among the Khasi and Nagas", in J.P.Singh and G. Sengupta (Eds) : *Archaeology of North Eastern India.* pp 106 – 125. New Delhi: Vikas Publishing House.

Shadap Sen, N.C., 1981, *The Origin and Early History of Khasi-Synteng.* Calcutta : Firma K. L. M. Pvt. Ltd.

18

The Indigenous Belief and Knowledge in the Meitei Lai Haraoba and its Relevance

K. Saratchandra Singh

The present chapter primarily attempts to elucidate a few relevant aspects of primordial human life and values latent in the Meitei Lai Haraoba, but not to give the details of the same.

Lai Haraoba is the ritualistic festival related with propitiation of the *Oomang Lais* of the Meitei and it is celebrated in the whole Manipur valley, where the Meiteis are widely inhabited. Etymologically *Lai Haraoba* means pleasing of the Gods or Goddesses or the merrymaking of the Gods and Goddesses as different scholars would express. A few scholars also suggests it originated from the term *Lai Hoi Laoba* which literally means shouting of *hoi* by the *Lais* or deity, while emerging out from within the person of *Atingkok Sidaba* (a name of Almighty) at the time of *Leishemba* (creation of the earth). The Meiteis believe in the worship of their ancestors and they used to maintain special locations as dwelling abodes of spirits of their progenitors. As such, places are associated with the solitude grove or sylvan localities, thus the deities are broadly known as *Oomang Lai* (*Oomang* = forest; *Lai* = God or deity).

Lai Haraoba festivals are celebrated for about a week with pomp and gaiety strictly following the ritual norms. However, it may be celebrated only for one day or sometimes, it may continue for about a month or so as in the case of *Moirang Thangjing Haraoba.*

By celebrating *Haraoba,* the Meiteis believed that the pleasure of the *Lais* (deities) is evoked and in return, the human beings are blessed with happiness and prosperity. Therefore, the rituals are essentially centered around to attempting to exalt the virtues of the *Taibangpanba Mapu* or the Supreme Almighty by re-enacting the works of His creation, His activities etc.

The rituals of the *Lai Haraoba* are performed by the professionals such as *Amaiba* (Priest), *Amaibi* (Priestess), and *Pena Khongba* (Musical player), who are recognised by the *Maiba-Maibi Loishang* (Institution of the Priest and Priestess) of the *Kornung* (Royal Palace).

The chief process of *Laibou Chongba* is a main component ritual of the *Lai Haraoba* for which a number of young and old of different age and sex groups participate. In this, the priestess perceivably depicts the creation of the earth, mimed the creation of the living beings- mainly the development process of the human body right from the mother's womb till the completion of the final human form in dance form. In doing so, the priestess with her loud voice depicts the creation processes, leading to birth of a child, making of different human body parts (*Hakchang saba*) in at least 64 ways of hand and body movements and gestures. Simultaneously, the chain of the participants in a very orderly way would follow every step of the head priestess. Subsequently, the construction of a house is also depicted.

Necessary arrangements of the *Lai Haraoba* festival are done by an authority, which is composed of one *Lai Shelungba, Laroi, Singloi, Leiroi, Choubon, Pakhanglakpa, Ningol-lakpa* and some other elders as members. This Body takes decision of the celebration of the festival and it is the responsibility of the *Lai Shelungba* and *Choubon* to invite *Amaiba* (Priest) and *Amaibi* (Priestess) and *Pena Khongba.*

There are four types of *Lai Haraoba,* namely – *Kanglei Haraoba, Chakpa Haraoba, Moirang Haraoba,* and *Kakching Haraoba*, depending on the sub-groups and territoriality etc.

Certain differences could be noticed as regards the ritual observance in all these four types of *Lai Haraoba,* although the general characteristics of the celebrations are fundamentally the same.

The whole process of *Lai Haraoba* may broadly be divided into seven parts.

***Laiphi Setpa* (the dressing of the deity)**

One day before the commencement of *Haraoba,* dressing and decoration of the images of the deities are done. Normally, there are two images – one for *Lainingthou* (male deity) and another for *Lairemma* (female deity). After the dressings are over, both the deities are ceremoniously placed on their respective thrones and the process is known as *Phamdengba.*

***Lai Eekouba* (calling the spirit of the deities)**

Lai Eekouba is the ritualistic act of calling up of the spirit or the soul of the deity from water, which may be from a nearby pond or a stream. The ritual is done near the water by the *Maibas, Maibis* and the *Penakhongba.* Two persons would carry *Eshaiphu* (pitcher), one each and they are known as *Laipuba* (deity bearer). They are followed by four girls – two of them carrying *Senkha* (*pan* box) and the other two carrying *Kaoshel Humai* (hand fan). A procession would go which is arranged according to the order of age group – elders are to lead, while the younger ones are to follow. After returning from the water site in procession, the main ritual part is the infusion or the transmission of the spirit of the deities into the images. Preceeding and following it, some other rituals are the making of offerings, *Laihou Jagoi* (opening/initiation dance), *Anam Athou Kokpa* (the rite of purification) and *Saroi Khangba* (feeding of the evil spirits) may be mentioned. Thereafter, the first day ends.

Daily Rituals

With the singing of the *Yakairol* (invocation) by the *Maiba* (priest) with the accompaniment of *Pena* (a traditional musical instrument of stringed fiddle), in the early morning, the daily programme begins. The *Laipao* or oracle by the *Maibis* (priestess) follows this. In the afternoon, a *Maibi* initiates the ritual of *Laibou-La-Thaba* in front of the shrine with a dance recital known as *Laihou Jagoi* (a beginning dance). Thereafter, *Lei Langba* (offering of flowers), *Laibou Jagoi*, and *Hoi Laoba* etc. are followed.

Laibou Jagoi may be considered as an important component of *Lai Haraoba*. In this dance, the Priest and Priestess with the accompaniment of the *Pena Khongba* in the lead, while the *Laipuba* (deity bearers), *Thang Paiba* (sword holders) and the participants – who are men and women of varying ages would join the encircling line in full traditional costumes. *Laibou Jagoi* consists of 364 *Khutheks* or hand movements and in this, it tries to convey the formation of different body parts, the birth of a child, construction of a house (*Yumsarol khuthek*), plantation of cotton, weaving of clothes and ultimately offering of the produces to the deity.

After the *Laibou Jagoi,* there follows the ritual of *Lairel Mathek Chatpa* (the dance depicting the never-ending creation of the Almighty) in which the line moves in a serpentine pattern. The rituals of *Hoi Laoba* or the shouting of *hoi* concludes the day.

Lai Nupi Thiba or *Kanglei Thokpa*

In this ritual, a *Maibi* would depict the search of a wife by *Lainingthou Khoriphaba*. The *Maibi* covers her face with a veil and holding a polo stick looks around moving round in a Trans and at last, a girl of choice from among the crowd would be hooked by the polo-stick. Thereafter, the girl shall have to come forward and dance with the *Maibi.*

Lai Lam Thokpa

On the evening of 5th, or 7th or 9th day of the festival, the deities are taken in procession to a particular open ground, where most of the daily ritual items are observed. After that, the deities are brought back to the shrine.

Sannaba or Games and Sport

Many traditional games such as *Mukna* (Meitei style wrestling), *Lamjel* (race), *Khong-Kangjei* (Meitei style hockey), *Thouri Chingnaba* (tug of war), *Yubi Lakpi* (snatching of coconut) and even S*agolkangjei* (Meitei style polo) are the important competitions held normally on the last but day of *Lai Haraoba.*

The Last day of the Festival

In the afternoon of the last day of the *Haraoba,* few rituals such as *thangthaba* (sword dance), which is performed by the *Maibis, Lairel-mathek* (serpentine pattern), *Hakchang saba* (creation of human body anatomy) etc are performed. In the late evening, an important ritual called as *Tangkhul Thokpa* (appearance of Tangkhul) – a form of dance drama describing the meeting of *Nongpok Ningthou* (dressed in a Tangkhul tribe) with *Panthoibi* (dressed in a Tangkhul girl) is performed. It is about the quarrel over a piece of land, hoeing the *jhum* field and finally about their reconciliation with a romantic note. After this, certain other important rituals such as *Ougri hangel, Thawaimi-konba* (embracing of soul), *Huithi-yenthi yeppa*, and *Sharit litpa* etc. are performed. Certain other ritual songs such as *Khencho, paosha, Hijing Herao* and *Uyanlol* are sung. These are followed by the rituals of *Lai Nong-gaba* (return of the deity back to heaven) and the ritual of *Lai tet haba* (appeasement of the deity). The whole process of *Lai Haraoba* is concluded with *Saroi Khangba* (feeding of evil spirits).

Significance

From the overall study of the whole process of Lai Haraoba, which has been described as the propitiation and worship of the Creator for His greatness and virtues for evolving the universe, the earth and its animate and inanimate, certain significant observations may be inferred.

Understanding the Nature: It indicates the understanding and importance of the five elements and properties of the Universe such as *Atingkok* (space), *Malangba* (atmosphere), *Laija* (water), *Meitreng* (heat) and *Malem* (earth), by the Progenitors. As per Meitei cosmogony, the creation of the universe and the earth has been symbolically re-enacted through rituals, prayers, dances and songs of the *Lai Haraoba* festival.

Understanding Human Physiology : *Lai Haraoba* conveys messages for the evolution of life, caring for the child, knowledge of different human anatomy, and body parts etc. It also symbolises concept of fertility of life.

Socio-cultural Aspect: From *Lai Haraoba,* people learn the art of living together, integrative and corporate life in a disciplined way based on the customs and laws of the community.

One can understand the people of the land used to practice *jhum* cultivation, knew cultivation of beans, rice and, banana etc. They also knew the art of systematic construction of houses with the use of bamboo and other materials since very ancient time.

The Art of Dance: Since very early days, the Meitei life was closely associated with different form of folk dances, which one feels as the sources of the foundation for more sophisticated forms of the present Manipuri classical dances.

Games and Sport as Way of Life : It may also undoubtedly be said that the people of Manipur had the tradition of taking interest in various games and sports, of which some are very much indigenous since early days. Besides, the Meitei *Thang-Ta* (*Thang* means sword and *Ta* means spear) which is the martial art has also been well recognised. The game of Polo has been claimed to originate from Manipur. The international style of Hockey and Wrestling appeared to be the modified and improved style of the traditional Meitei style *Khong Kangjei* and the *Meitei Mukna* respectively.

In a way, it may be said that the *Lai Haraoba* festival, which is widely celebrated almost in all the Meitei localities and villages still has relevance with the day-to-day life of the present day Meitei society.

References

Paratt, S.N., 1980, *Religion of Manipur.* Calcutta.

Ratnakumar, K., 2001, *Lai Haraoba of Manipur.* Imphal: Lamyanba Printers, Konung Lampak.

Singh, M.K., 1950, *Religious Developments in Manipur in the 18th and 19th Centuries*. State Kala Academy: Bhagyabati Karyalaya, Churachand Printing Works.

Singh, M.K., 1988, *Religion of Manipur.* Delhi: Manas Publications.

Singh, W.L., 1989, *Lai Haraoba.* Imphal: R. B. Printing House.

INDEX